TRANSFER OF EDUCATION LEADERSHIP TRAINING SKILLS

TRANSFER OF EDUCATION LEADERSHIP TRAINING SKILLS

MAKING IT HAPPEN

MAINA WAGÍOKÒ

PARTRIDGE

To order additional copies of this book, contact
Toll Free 0800 990 914 (South Africa)
+44 20 3014 3997 (outside South Africa)
orders.africa@partridgepublishing.com

www.partridgepublishing.com/africa

Table of Contents

Transfer of Educational Leadership and Management Training Skills in School Governance in a Coastal County of Kenya

Prologue

Stakeholders have been urging Headteachers to attend professional learning session (PLS) so as to improve school leadership. The assumptions have been that if the Headteachers are trained they will be able to govern their schools effectively and hence the National Examination Performance (NEP) trends will increase. Investments have been put into PLS. Despite the effort the NEP has been on the decline. This has led to blame game between stakeholders and Headteachers. This study aimed at exploring experiences of the Headteachers as they transfer their education leadership and management training (ELMT) skills into practice. The exploration included identifying levels of implementation, Headteachers' perspectives on Newstrom's barriers and the barriers Headteachers identified and how they managed them. Exploration, business management skills were also analyzed to understand how they can be infused in school governance to manage transfer of ELMT skill barriers. A qualitative and explorative case study approach was implemented where a total of 40 Headteachers from schools in the county of Mombasa, Kenya were profiled some four years and others three years after attending ELMT. The NEP trends were analyzed and schools with improving NEP trends were identified for deeper analysis. Four Headteachers, 12 teachers were interviewed from the schools with improving NEP trends. Data was collected through structured forms, interviews, observation and artifact analysis. The data was analyzed thematically. Triangulation of data was made from multiple sources for reliability and validity. The finding showed Headteachers were implementing slightly above half but less than two thirds of the content they were taught four/three years after ELMT training. The Headteachers implemented concepts that they had good or excellent understanding either occasionally or always. The barriers that the Headteachers experienced were teachers, policy, resources, stakeholders and students. The Headteachers' action before, during and after the training also influenced their transfer of ELMT. The Headteachers perspectives on barriers were informed by the contextual structures and experiences such as school population, catchment areas and self-disposition. The Headteachers efforts to overcome the barriers on transfer of ELMT skill to practice included managing change, involving stakeholders, managing resources and motivation. All these approaches could be supplemented by business management skills such as hotspots, effective teams, stakeholder's involvement, advanced human resource management, project and process management. Other concepts that could assist the Headteachers, though not identified by the Headteachers, included strategic management, outsourcing and use of technology, performance management and advanced financial management. The transfer of skills is the responsibility of the Headteachers, the management (Ministry of Science and Technology (MoEST) and Teachers Service commission (TSC) and the organization designing the training and the trainers. All the responsible people must be aware of their contribution to the transfer of ELMT through their roles and responsibilities and make efforts to perform and support the transfer of ELMT skills.

Key Words: transfer of skills, training, barriers, school governance

Acknowledgements

I wish to acknowledge my family Nancy Njoki Mwangi, Joseck Gioko Maina, Elikanah Mwangi Maina and Mum Mary Nduta Gioko for their support during the time of my study. I also wish to thank my line managers Mr. Rupen Chande and Mr. Jonathon Marsh for their support during the research. Special dedication goes to Mr. Rob Burrough who was instrumental in facilitating my access to the course. The county directorate team of both TSC (Dr. Rugut Ibrahim) and MoEST (Mr. Abdikadir Kike). My project team (Ms. Rose Iminza, Mr. Howard Omukami and Mr. Enos Kiforo) and our driver Mr. Kent Muinde who were very instrumental during the field data collection work for making it happen in a collaborative and supportive approach. Finally Literacy coach Ms. Rosemary Waga and Tutor Ms. Grace Alwala for the transcription and editorial work.

List of Figures

List of Tables

List of Abbreviations

ABC	Activity Based Costing
AKAM	Aga Khan Academy, Mombasa
AKU	Aga Khan University
BMC	Business Management Course
BOM	Board of Management
BSC	Balanced Scorecard
CD	Compact Disk
COP	Community of practice
CP	Course Participant
ECD	Early Childhood Development
ELM	Educational leadership and management
ELMT	Educational leadership and management training
EO	Entrepreneurial Orientation
EVA	Economic Value Added
FPE	Free Primary Education
GC	Guidance and Counseling
HR	Human Resource
HT	Headteacher
ICT	Information and Communication Technology
IT	Information Technology
ITP	Internal Teacher Practice
KCPE	Kenya Certificate of Primary Education
KEMI	Kenya Education Management Institute
KEPSHA	Kenya Primary School Headteachers Association
KICD	Kenya Institute of Curriculum Development
KNEC	Kenya National Examination Council
KNUT	Kenya National Union of Teachers
MoEST	Ministry of Education Science and Technology
NA	Not Applicable
NEP	National Examination Performance
NPDP	New Product Development Program
OC	Organizational Culture

PIB	Perspective in Barriers
PLN	Professional Learning Network
PLS	Professional Learning sessions
PM	Project Management
PTA	Parents Teachers Association
QASO	Quality Assurance and Standards Officer
SC	School Culture
SDP	School Development Plan
SWOT	Strengths, Weaknesses, Opportunities and Threats
SIMSC	School Instruction Material Selection Committee
TPM	Traditional Project Management
TSC	Teachers Service Commission
TUC	Trade union Congress

Dedication

To the children of Kenya and the world, my efforts have been to do what I can to ensure you are facilitated to realize your potential, I will not rest.

Chapter 1: Overview

Chapter one provides an overview of the study and discusses the problem of school leadership, management and the current blame game on declining National Examination Performance (NEP) trends. Based on this, research questions were raised to assess the transfer of Education leadership and management training (ELMT) on school governance. Explorative case study, qualitative approach provided a deeper analysis of the identified NEP trends, to explore how the Headteachers transferred their ELMT skills to school governance. The significance of the study was to gain insights on the levels of ELMT skills implementation, Headteachers' perspective on barriers and their identified barriers and how the Headteachers managed the barriers with the possibility of infusing aspects of Business Management Course (BMC) to facilitate effective ELMT skills transfer to school governance. The findings will inform future planning, implementation and follow-up support of ELMT and any other professional learning session (PLS) for school leaders and managers for effective transfer of the skills.

Many school Headteachers were promoted to the positions of leadership without formal leadership training. The roles and the responsibilities of the Headteachers in a school were to lead learning as pedagogical leaders. According to Wango (2009), the quality of education could be enhanced through improved school administration and management. Current research shows that the leadership of a school is a critical factor in turning around low-achieving schools (Crew, 2007; Norguera & Wang, 2006). The leadership could be enhanced by attending professional learning sessions. There are several factors which influence the transfer of training and they include the trainee, the school culture and the managers among others (Newstrom, 1986). These factors influence how the training skills are transferred to school governance. Complete transfer could influence school governance which may lead to an impact on the NEP trends. The complex natures of schools require leaders to have the ability to be thoughtful and thorough, as well as courageous, humble, and emphatic in order to address these multifaceted challenges.

One of the measures of quality of teaching and learning was indirectly linked to the NEP. To facilitate the roles and responsibilities of Headteachers, the Ministry of Education Science and technology (MoEST), Teachers Service Commission (TSC) and non –governmental organizations such as Aga Khan Academies Unit have come up with PLS such as ELMT for the Headteachers. ELMT also focuses on cultivating habits, raising self-awareness and reflections as well as helping Headteachers identify areas of improvement (Allen, 2007). This study explores the transfer of ELMT skills to school governance in Mombasa County in Kenya.

The school as an organization can build the capacity of Headteachers, to deal with work related issues, by developing and implementing formal training policies and programs. However, unless these programs include strategies to develop co-teachers' support for the ELMT content and objectives, effective training transfer will fail to occur (Blednick & Wilson, 2011). An effective PLS will result not only in increased knowledge, skills and abilities, but also their application to school governance (Tucker & Stronge, 2005). Effective ELMT skills transfer is therefore evident when the knowledge, skills and abilities acquired during the ELMT context, produce the desired behavioral change in school governance.

Problem Statement

To ensure that Headteachers are equipped with knowledge, skills, and abilities to perform their duties effectively by attending in-service training such as ELMT. The Headteachers are strongly encouraged to take PLS by MoEST and TSC for reasons such as training, promotion and the need for new knowledge, skills and abilities.

The Kenya National Examination Council (KNEC) (2012) reports that, National Examination mean grade between 0-250 marks have been decreasing at a rate of -0.246 in the last five years. The discrepancy in the trends is contrary to the expected outcome after the Headteachers have attended ELMT. NEP in primary school has become the key aspect of measuring school performance. Educational leadership and its development are essential in improving school performance, hence raising educational standards (Wango, 2009). Current research shows that the leadership of a school is a critical factor in turning around low-achieving schools (Crew, 2007; Norguera & Wang, 2006). The leadership is enhanced by attending professional learning sessions. There are several factors which influence the transfer of training and they include the trainee, the school culture and the managers among others (Newstrom, 1986). These factors influence how the training skills are transferred to school governance. Complete transfer will influence school governance which may lead to an impact on the National Examination Trends. The complex nature of schools requires leaders to have the ability to be thoughtful and thorough, as well as courageous, humble, and emphatic in order to address these multifaceted challenges. On the other hand, NEP is high stakes, as it determines the ranking of schools both at district, county and national levels. It also determines the students' transition to secondary and measures the effectiveness of school governance. NEP trends among other factors are thus correlated to the effectiveness of school governance by the Headteachers. Meanwhile, being a Headteacher is based on either being an exemplary teacher, maturation in the profession, knowing someone in the administration, attending PLS or excelling in an extra-curricular event (Ministry of Education, 2008). Based on the identified basis of becoming a Headteacher, the only professional capacity building approach was through PLS; otherwise the position was attained without any education leadership and managerial training. Both the current status of NEP trends and the headship appointments have prompted MoEST and TSC to advise the Headteachers to attend PLS such as ELMT. The reason for the advice was to empower the Headteachers, to govern their schools effectively and as a result improve on NEP. Burke and Hutchins (2008) observe that organizations today strive for knowledgeable and skilled employees in order to improve organizational performance. However the NEP trends were not indicative of the MoEST and TSC expectations. The dismissal NEP trends were still occurring even after the Headteachers had attended PLS such as ELMT. According to Cheng and Hampson (2008) most successful training programmes fail to transfer knowledge and new skills to learners. From the observations by the researcher, some Headteachers had returned to pre-ELMT practice, having earned a certificate and/or promotion, others have become effective school governors as a result of ELMT. Cheng and Hampson (2008) further identify the epitome of any learning outcome as the idea of the training needs being demonstrably effective. The differences in effectiveness have become a serious issue to the extent that the TSC has directed that school Headteachers' tenure in office be pegged on the NEP trends and that any Headteacher who doesn't attend a PLS within two years risks losing the teaching license or being demoted. Notwithstanding the complexity of training, according to Cheng (2008) and Hampson it is disputable that the true success of training is represented in the learner's ability to demonstrate what is learned.

The rush to attend PLS has been interpreted by MoEST as mainly for the sole purpose of acquiring papers rather than skills for competency (Ministry of Education, 2008). This was contrary to the assumptions by the MoEST and TSC that PLS was usually designed and implemented so as to empower the Headteachers with appropriate skills for effective governance of their schools (Ministry of Education, 2008). The Headteachers and the MoEST appeared to be conflicting on the purpose of PLS.

On the other hand, Headteachers had decried the quality of the PLS they were asked to attend (Gioko, 2011). Gioko (2013) acknowledges the design of the PLS as one element that influences the uptake and sustainability of the skills learnt. Moreover, Newstrom (1986) identified several factors known to affect the transfer of training. These included: individual learners, training programs, work environment, trainee's immediate manager/supervisor. Although the levels of transfer of the ELMT skills were not known yet, the information on whether this transfer was effective in schools with improving NEP trends was of crucial importance to all education stakeholders. This study aimed to explore how the Headteachers transferred the ELMT skills they were exposed to in the governance of their schools. It also sought to develop a deeper understanding of what exactly the Headteachers implemented. Further, the study analyzed how business management skills could be infused in the transfer of ELMT skills. The outcomes will inform how to design future school leaders' preparation programmes for effective school governance.

The problem is that a lot of money and time is invested to train the Headteachers so as they can improve the NEP trends through effective school governance. However the NEP trends are still on decline and there is no evidence on the level of implementation of the ELMT skills to school governance. The school managers expect improved results; the Headteachers blame the managers for demanding them to attend ELMT. There is no information of the Headteachers experience on transfer of ELMT skills on school governance.

Purpose of Research

This study was aimed at exploring how Headteachers transfer their ELMT skills to school governance 4 years after attending the training session. The purpose also enabled the exploration of how the skills learnt in BMC, can be implemented in school governance. Furthermore, the outcome of the research will be used to develop structures that will facilitate the Headteachers before, during and after ELMT to create an enabling environment for transfer of skills to school governance.

Empirical studies repeatedly show that good leadership development interventions promote organizational performance (Avolio, Avey, & Quisenberry, 2010); this is the case across a broad array of organization types, leadership models and management levels (Avolio, Reichard, Hannah, Walumbwa, & Chan, 2009). However, the ELM cohorts were displaying differing results in performance, hence the need to identify the level of implementation of ELMT skills. The implementation of the ELMT skills was expected to impact on leadership and management in the school hence reflecting on school governance. Research to date reveals that learning and development programmes are not achieving their full potential in effecting performance change (Leimbach, 2010), and may in part be due to the complexities involved in translating knowledge derived from training to workplace applications (Holton, Voller, Schofield, & Devine, 2010). The research revelation needs to be verified for the ELM cohorts which are demonstrating improving NEP trends. Based on the seminal study by Saks and Belcourt (2006), self-reports place estimates of the amount of new skills that are still in use 12 months after a typical training event at only about 35%. Such a situation has contributed to the need to track the levels of transfers of ELMT skills to school governance for possible yielding of long term effects (Avolio, Avey, & Quisenberry, 2010).

Headteachers exposed to ELMT are expected to put to practice the aspects that were included in the course outline. The implementation of these aspects was aimed at improving the leadership and management hence effective school governance which may influence NEP trends. Tracking the implementation will give an indicator on how the transfer of ELMT skills is happening in school governance. Within the distinctive settings of curriculum, school calendar, empowering Headteachers and declining NEP trends, a great amount of time and money is invested in training (Noe, Hollenbeck, Gerhart, & Wright, 2006; Velada, Caetano, Michel, & Kavanagh, 2007). Therefore, the level of transfer can indicate a return of investment.

The evaluation of ELMT skills transfer offers a valuable tool for the systematic collection of data regarding the success of ELMT (Goldstein, 1986). Evaluations by the study addressed two major categories: outcomes and process evaluations (Russon & Reinelt, 2004). Outcome evaluations will determine whether and to what extent the expected results (in these cases ELMT skills occurred as a result of training) were realized. Process evaluation will seek to understand why the intended outcomes did or did not occur. By addressing outcomes and processes, programme evaluation can be used to form judgments about ELMT effectiveness, and the empirical findings can be used to review ELMT. The evaluation could further help to identify the most cost-effective ELMT design among other delivering similar content, as well as guide resource allocation by formulating ELMT with the most desirable impact on target audiences.

Significance of the Study

This study is the first formal study conducted in connection with ELM course, offered at the Aga Khan Academy Mombasa, to Mombasa and Kwale county School Leaders. The results of this study will serve as a foundation to conduct more extensive studies with the project manager, facilitators, graduates and current course participants of ELM course. This study will contribute to educational research in the areas of course design, leadership training, school management and educational communities of practice for school support programmes.

There is a need to understand the transfer of ELMT skills in school governance so as to understand how to design ELMT and to track the return of investment. School leadership unlike many other organizations, is considered to be an essential service which requires school leaders to be on the cutting edge and equipped with the ability to implement best practices. On this premise, transfer of training is crucial in school governance and knowing how it happens successfully in the schools will identify ways of facilitating the transfer. The findings will have significant implications for the design and implementation of Headteachers' training programs and policies. One conclusion that emerges from a review of this research is that training is paramount to the effectiveness of training and education programs.

Benchmarking the ELMT skill transfer against competitors served as a catalyst for debate of what the stakeholders really value (Bowman & Schoenberg, 2008). Offering value in ELMT skill transfer will depend on the knowledge of the target course participants by understanding their needs and how they evaluate different product offerings (Bowman & Schoenberg, 2008). The target groups were teachers in school, parents and the community. According to Hamels work, the Headteachers will need to re-conceive the existing models of school governance in a way that will create value and offer opportunities to the stakeholders (Bowman and Schonberg, 2008). The knowledge of the skills possessed and the projected stakeholders' demands will offer leverage during the ELMT skill transfer design. Bowman and Schoenberg (2008) demand the importance of understanding the criteria the stakeholder's uses to evaluate the ELMT skill transfer. Furthermore, knowing the stakeholders' perception and experiences on ELMT skill transfer and cost will enhance competitive positioning (Bowman & Schoenberg). Bowman and Schonberg advice that systematic exploration of stakeholders' needs, perception and continuous listening to stakeholders could lead to the discovery of what is valued in the ELMT skill transfer and the services and what could be done to improve the perceived use value. Stakeholder's evaluation and feedback was undertaken as a strategic development from the demand side (Bowman & Schoenberg, 2008). Bowman and Schoenberg (2008) suggest that unconstructive buildup of stakeholder's perception of the ELMT skill transfer performance and the competitors will guide the competitive strategy of winning the ELMT sessions in the stakeholder's eyes –perceived use value and price.

The approaches will also bring opportunities of understanding how to infuse the knowledge learnt in BMC to ELMT to make it more effective and highly impacting. Meeting the objectives of the ELMT is very crucial. Substantial finance and time resources have been used by MoEST and other non-governmental institutions to plan and offer PLS. For example, the ELMT objectives are to improve education standards in respective schools. Hence, it is important to understand the factors that influence the achievement of the objectives, as well as realize the return on investment (ROI). Headteachers have been seen as key in managing change in their schools for improvement. Hence, the research results informed the transfer of ELMT skills in school governance to facilitate increasing NEP trends. It also helped to understand how the knowledge gained from the management course could be infused into the ELMT to offer more effective knowledge, skills and values for school Headteachers. Insights informed ways of revising the ELMT, to ensure an improved success rate. With an opportunity to train over 300 Headteachers in the coastal counties, developing an effective model of training might attract MoEST to buy-in and take-up to over 32,000 Headteachers country wide (AKFC, 2011). Therefore, it's important to come up with ELMT which is effective and has high impact on school governance. The exploration brought insights on how timelines influence implementation practices. It also identified the aspects of training which have been sustained over time. Furthermore, the exploration brought forth adaptations on skills offered. This information will be crucial in designing ELMT as well as exploring structures to support the implementation of ELMT skills. At the moment, MoEST through Kenya Education Management Institute (KEMI) has initiated a training endeavor on educational leadership and management for all the Headteachers in primary schools. The findings of this research will be instrumental in influencing policy on ELMT. Currently, there are no studies that explore the transfer of ELMT skills in school governance. On this note, it is imperative that training institutions shared should provide sufficient evidence that the training efforts are being fully utilized (Hunter-Johnson & Closson, 2011; Velada et al., 2007). Having concrete solutions in mind to handle potential barriers to change makes it more likely that leaders will translate their learning into action back at the workplace (Suinn, 1990).

The findings of this study expanded the body of knowledge about barriers of training transfer for Headteachers. The study reinforced the importance of overcoming challenges, through innovative and reflective practices to implement the skills acquired in school governance.

The goal of this study was to help contribute to the body of practices and strategies for schools across the county. The insights gained from documenting and exploring the transfer of skills in school governance was instrumental in identifying how the Headteachers overcome the barriers. As part of this study, opportunities were also explored on how to infuse business management skills in school governance training modules. The findings also served as testimonials and inspiration for aspiring Headteachers working in similar contexts.

Last and most importantly, this study served as evidence of the possibilities and as a promise to stakeholders that entrust their Headteachers to attend PLS. There are Headteachers who are willing to implement the skills learnt in school governance for the improvement of NEP trends but they need to be skilled on how to overcome the barriers they will face on re-entry in the schools.

Research Design

The study aimed to explore the transfer of ELMT skills to school governance. The study probed deeply and analyzed intensively the multifarious phenomenon (Cohen & Manion, 2000) that constituted school governance and how it was influenced by the ELMT skills and aspects of BMC. School governance was approached from a dialectical perspective meaning both the person and the environment will be taken into consideration (Valsiner & Van de Veer, 2000). Data is strong in reality; hence the study examined an instant action within a bounded system (Bassey, 1999; Cohen & Manion, 2000; Walker, 1983). This involved transfer of ELMT skills to school governance. The study was done in schools where the Headteachers had attended ELMT, and the NEP trends were improving post-ELMT because it afforded an excellent opportunity to discover phenomena within the real world settings in which they occurred (Merriam, 1998b). This study was an instrumental case study, as it examined this particular case to provide an insight into issues of transfer of ELMT skills on school governance. The researcher had an in-depth look at the case, scrutinized its contents and action in details, these helped him to understand school governance.

The study was also explorative in nature, the first goal sought to seek information from the Headteachers' perceptions, actions, the artifacts, documents, or tools they use, views on effectiveness, possibilities and constraints, thoughts of teachers under the Headteachers, and the description of the culture in which the Headteachers govern, to develop a holistic understanding of the case. The second goal began with a predetermined set of questions, related to transfer of skills. An evolving working hypothesis emerged (Merriam, 1998b), new questions were asked based on what the observations, data, and inferences suggested. As naturalistic research continued, it was uncommon to change direction and ask new questions (Merriam, 1998b). It would have been naive to assume all possible questions could be asked at the outset because of the constantly evolving system that occurs in any school.

The study was an enquiry, in real life context, where deep investigation involved interdependence of parts and the patterns that emerged (Bassey, 1999; Yin, 2009). Furthermore, the nature of the study relied on multiple sources of evidence, with data needing to converge in a triangulation fashion as a result benefit from prior development of theoretical proposition to guide data collection and analysis (Yin, 2009). In this study, the researcher explored a single phenomenon, which is contemporary with real-life context (Rossman & Rallis, 1998; Yin, 2009). Therefore, the study was a qualitative, instrumental, exploratory and interpretive case study.

Research Questions

This study sought to determine the experiences of Headteachers as they transferred ELMT skills to school governance in the primary education system in a county at the coastal region of Kenya 4 years after attending the program. The research questions were:

1. To what extent has the ELMT skills been transferred to school governance four years after attending ELMT?
2. What are the Headteachers' perspectives on identified barriers on transfer of skills?
3. What barriers are experienced by Headteachers as they transfer their skills into school governance?
4. How do Headteachers overcome the barriers they face during the transfer of the ELMT skills?

Assumptions and Limitations

For the purpose of this study it is assumed that:

- All the Headteachers who attended the ELMT will be implementing the knowledge and skills in school governance.
- NEP is an indicator of quality education.
- Quality education is facilitated by effective school governance.
- Education leadership and management skills are acquired through training.
- The training the Headteachers attended contributed to school governance.
- The respondents were honest to the questions asked.
- The changes in the NEP trends in schools are as a result of effective school governance.
- Debates on poor NEP results, incapable Headteachers and ineffective ELMT could be addressed when the transfer of skills are identified and matched to the results.

Delimitations

Delimitations are the boundaries set forth by the researcher to narrow the scope and provide parameters for the study (Creswell, 2003). This study was delimited to exploring transfer of ELMT skills to school governance.

Graduates of the ELMT who hold current Headteacher positions were involved in the study. Therefore, generalization of the results from this study to ELM programs and Headteachers in other geographic areas may not be reasonable. Conclusions are limited to transfer of training with similar demographic with emphasis on school governance.

Limitations are weaknesses which are beyond the researcher's control (Cromwell & Kolb, 2003). Limitations can also impact generalizability. Being a former faculty, recent coordinator and current head of the professional development center, the former patron of the graduate's alumni chapter and having personal life experiences involving school governance, the researcher encountered bias and had prejudgments when collecting and analyzing data, resulting in a limitation of the study. However, the researcher had an extensive background in conducting highly sensitive and confidential audits that require a high regard for ethics and integrity; therefore, the researcher was aware of such influence and its impacts. To mitigate and limit the influence of bias, the researcher used multiple sources of information for triangulation and clarity of what was happening.

Another limitation for the study was the small population and sample size. The study focused on Headteachers four years after attending ELMT, only 40 out of the 65 ELM trainees in the county met the Headteachers' threshold. The final limitation was the profile questionnaire and the Headteachers' availability and willingness to participate in the initial profile questionnaire, if selected to participate in the interviews and respond to the questionnaires, allow shadowing classroom observation and teachers to fill in the questionnaires on Headteachers' leadership, and the team spirit in the school. Due to the busy schedule of the Headteachers, their time was very limited. Requesting participation in all these, posed some challenges that may have impacted the response rate.

Despite this the researcher tried to minimize the impact of these limitations to data collection. Since the research was a case study, the generalizability of the findings was not predetermined. A thick description of the process was achieved through use of multiple sources. The thick description enabled readers to determine the degree fit between their situation and the presented description which could increase the possibility of transfer (Lincon & Guba, 2000).

Operational Definitions

Business Management Course - These are concepts, ideas and theories learnt during the business management coursework (SMCU, 2013).

Course Participant CP- a Headteacher who has attended ELMT for a period of six months (AKAM, 2013).

Governance – This is the pedagogical leadership, which is used to govern the school to ensure participation, placement and effective use of resources in the school leadership and management so as to have an effective learning environment producing high performing students (AKAM, 2013).

Headteacher – This term is used to refer to the head of a school. Headteachers will be referred to as the pedagogical leaders of the school. These are the course participants for the ELMT. This is the person in charge of the running of the school appointed by TSC, supported by MoEST, the Board of Management (BOM) and Parents teachers Association (PTA) (Ministry of Education, 2008).

National Examination –This is the Exit examination in class 8 of primary school. It is a high stake examination as it ranks schools, offers progression to secondary school and scholarship opportunities (KNEC, 2013).

NEP- National examination performance is the mean score earned by a school after sitting national examinations prepared and marked by KNEC (Ministry of Education, 2008).

Professional learning session – this is a session attended by an individual to expose, offer and guide the individual on professional knowledge, skills, values and attitudes (AKAM, 2013).

School – An institution registered by MoEST, recognized and staffed by TSC to offer the national curriculum to students from a certain catchment area. It has a physical presence with facilities, resources, support staff and teachers to support teaching, learning and assessment (Ministry of Education, 2008).

Summary

This thesis is a study of the extent of transfer of ELMT skills on school governance, in the coastal county of Kenya. School governance has an influence on NEP. NEP has been used as a measure of quality of teaching and learning in schools. NEP is high stakes as it determines the transition of the students to secondary schools, ranking of the schools and potential scholarship offers. Headteachers' competencies determine the governance in schools. Most Headteachers are promoted to their post, either through experiences on the job or being exemplary teachers. This has prompted MoEST to urge the Headteachers to attend PLS. However, despite attending ELMT which is one of the PLS, a blame game has resulted with MoEST not observing the expected NEP trends and the Headteachers blaming the quality of the PLS. This study took an exploration of transfer of ELMT skills, to analyze how the skills are implemented in school governance. The research was triggered to identify the impact of transfer of skills to school governance and incorporated the aspects of management course, for designing high impact ELMT.

An explorative and instrumental qualitative case study approach was implemented in this research, 40 primary school Headteachers at the coastal county were used for profiling to identify the schools for the research. The Headteachers responded to a questionnaire form which was used to identify the pre - and post-ELMT NEP trends. Four Headteachers (2 male and 2 female) were then identified for the qualitative case study. 3 teachers from each school each from lower, middle and upper brought to 12 the number of teachers interviewed. Several tools were used to identify leadership styles and school learning environments. Open-ended questions, semi-structured interviews, observation schedules and artifact review protocol were used to obtain qualitative data. The research was undertaken with assumptions and delimitations.

Chapter 2: Literature review

This chapter reviews literature on transfer of training skills, exploring the factors influencing the transfer of different times before, during and after the training and identifies barriers to transfer of skills. The chapter brings to fore BMC skills which could be used to overcome the barriers and revitalize the transfer of ELMT skills to school governance.

Training and development is an integral component to the growth and development of any school (Hunter-Johnson, 2012). However, often time's organizations do not factor transfer of training as a part of the learning or training process. Despite this exclusion or oversight, transfer of training is indeed a continuation of the learning process. Transfer of training as affirmed by Baldwin and Ford (1988) "is the degree to which trainees effectively apply the knowledge, skills and attitudes gained in the training context to the job" (p. 63). The concept of transfer of training is crucial in any interdisciplinary academic, technical or professional setting.

One of the foremost issues is how Headteachers decide on the skills and behaviors that characterize good leadership and how they are developed. The Headteachers were exposed to a dearth of information, skills and knowledge hence the need to understand how they made decisions during implementation. Several factors including contextual realities, setting, task, role and time influence the interpretation of effective leadership (Hannum, Martineau, & Reinelt, 2007). ELMT explores different types of leadership styles hence exposing the Headteachers to a variety of leadership styles. The exposure poses a challenge to the Headteachers as to what to change to become more effective. Hence, one imperative aspect of transfer of training is to understand how perspectives influenced the transfer of skills.

Like financial commitment, time also plays a crucial role as it relates to investment in training and transfer of training. With the progression of research related to transfer of training, there has been a constant discussion regarding the lapse in time to apply what was learned and the amount of knowledge diminishing over that period (Bladwin & Ford, 1988). This study tracked Headteachers four years after attending ELMT. Initially, Baldwin and Ford (1988) contended that 10% of knowledge learned while in the training environment, is actually applied to the work environment. Newstrom (1986) had earlier graduated the transfer levels at 40% immediately, 25% six months later and 15% after one year. However, there are other researchers who suggest that 10 to 15 % of knowledge is actually applied to the work environment (Broad & Newstrom, 1992; Burke & Baldwin, 1999b). Apart from the percentages of skills transferred there was also an element of the percentage number of trainees that transferred the skills into practice. According to Saks (2002) 40% of trainees fail to transfer immediately after training, 70% falter in transfer one year after the training program and only 50% of training investment results in organizational or individual (Headteacher) improvement. Later on it was established that the percentages vary with time as Saks and Belcourt (2006) results indicate that 62%, 44%, and 34% of employees transfer immediately, six months, and one year after training, respectively. The average of these three values is 47% meaning that in Saks and Belcourt research almost half of the people trained transfer their training skills within a year. Although there is no indicators of the level of transfer four years after the training, the percentages gives a direction of a possible relationship between the lapse time and rates of transfer.

In this study 10% of the trainees were sampled hence Saks and Belcourt percentages cannot be compared as they refer to percentage of training implementing the skill and not the levels of implementation. Other researchers and practitioners concur that knowledge is diminished due to the time lapse in the application of knowledge to the work environment (Velada et al, 2007). This study will assess the extent of implementing the skills to school governance four years after attending ELMT.

The transfer of the exposed skills to practice varies because of typical barriers. Comprehension of the ELMT skills transfer will expose the barriers enabling possible efforts to remove, diminish, convert to positive forces or counter by balancing forces (Newstrom, 1986). A force field analysis could be used to determine what is against their implementation and what is for (Nugent, 2002). There are two aspects to this full transfer of training. The first is that trainees immediately apply all they learned in the training to their jobs, at least as well as they could demonstrate those skills at the end of the training program. This is the exit behavior at the end of the training. Second, with practice on the job, the trainees' level of skills will increase as they learn from what they have implemented.

The study sought to explore the barriers the Headteachers were facing as they transferred ELMT skills to school governance. Newstrom (1986) identified and ranked nine barriers of transfer to training (Table 1).

Table 1 *Ranked barriers to Transfer of training*

Rank Order	Barriers
1	Lack of reinforcement on the job
2	Interference from immediate environment (work, time pressures, insufficient authority, ineffective work processes, inadequate equipment and facilities).
3	Non-supportive organizational culture (no strong philosophical support for the goals of professional development programs).
4	Trainees' perception of impractical training programs.
5	Trainees' perception of irrelevant training content.
6	Trainees' discomfort with change and associated effort (undue discomfort or extra effort).
7	Separation from inspiration or support of the trainer.
8	Trainees' perception of poorly designed/delivered training.
9	Pressure from peers to resist changes (not transfer training to the workplace).

Key: 1 = greatest barrier; 9 = lowest barrier

Note. From "Leveraging Management Development through the Management of Transfer". By J. W. Newstrom, 1986, *Journal of Management Development, 5*(5), 33 - 45.

According to Newstrom (1986) the greatest barriers (rank 1-2-3) indicate that theoretical views of leadership needed to provide a consistent message in terms of organizational policies and practices so as to foster employee commitment to the mandate. The management has the potential to influence the leadership message and ensure congruency. Systems thinking analysts are credited for the saying, structure drives behavior. When the behaviors addressed by development programs are the same as those being rewarded at the workplace, and the expectations of both superiors and subordinates about effective leadership are aligned, leaders will have more incentive and find it easier to demonstrate their ELMT skills, resulting in the sustained behavioral change that is desired (Quinones, Ford, Sego, & Smith, 1995).

Newstrom's least barriers (rank 4-5-6-8) boil down to the leadership philosophy endorsed by the organization to guide leadership development. TSC and MoEST may be in the best position to describe the core elements of good leadership for the schools. The more clearly these set of beliefs and behaviors are articulated, the more likely Headteachers are to understand the standards being upheld, as well as how they are faring against the benchmark's set. This clarity may increase perceived relevance of recommended leadership programmes, and raise the probability that they will bring their learning back to the workplace (Quinones, 1995). The focus was on the Headteachers' understanding of different aspects of leadership and their practical implementation in school governance. The research compared Newstrom's rankings to the Headteachers' ranking. The two rankings were analyzed to check if there were congruency and what might have influenced any divergence. The exploration of the understanding could be matched with the actual implementation.

The least impacting barrier is peer support which is not categorized in the two groups. Burke and Hutchins (2008) offer a model to support transfer of training. They advocate for the stakeholder to include peers. According to Burke and Hutchins peer support has a significant influence on the effects of transfer. Hawley and Bernard (2005) observe peer collaboration, networking and sharing of ideas relating to the content to act as support for skills transfer. It will be important to compare the Headteachers' ranking and perspective of peer support in the transfer of training

The barriers to training vary on impacts based on the timelines that is before, during or after the ELMT. The research explored the Headteachers' perception on the impact of the barriers during the different ELMT timelines. Broad and Newstrom (1992) compared to Newstrom's (1986) findings had identified the effect of the barriers based on the timings namely before, during and after (Table 2)

Table 2 *Timing of Barriers to Transfer*

Before	During	After	Barrier
		1	Lack of reinforcement on the job
	2	1	Interference from immediate (work) environment
1	2	2	Non supportive organizational culture
	1		Trainee's perception of impractical training programs
	1		Trainee's perception of irrelevant training content
2	2	1	Trainee's discomfort with change and associated effort
		1	Separation from inspiration or support of the trainer
	1		Trainee's perception of poorly designed/ delivered training.
2		1	Pressure from peers to resist changes.

Key: 1 = primary time of impact; 2 = secondary time of impact

Note. The table classifies each of the nine major barriers to transfer into the most likely (indicated by 1), and the second most likely (indicated by 2) time period in which that barrier will arise.

From "Leveraging Management Development through the Management of Transfer". By J. W. Newstrom, 1986, *Journal of Management Development, 5*(5), 33 - 45.

Although Newstrom (1986) has categorized the impacts of transfer along timelines (Before, during and after) Burke and Hutchins (2008) argue that the transfer is not necessarily time bound and the barriers are not rooted in specific time phases hence the remedies should not be either. Baldwin-Evans (2006) and Clarke (2004) recommend supporting the training throughout the phases so as to extend beyond the training and promote for continuous on-job learning

Newstrom's barriers were interpreted by Griffin and Allen (2002) (Table 3) so as to be aligned with the Headteachers' responses. The interpretation would allow the alignment of the responses from the respondents,

Table 3 *Interpretation of the transfer of training barriers*

Barriers	Interpretation through the responses of the teachers and Headteachers
Lack of reinforcement on the job	Nobody cares if you do it or not
Interference from immediate (work) environment	Pulled in many directions
Non supportive organizational culture	The school does things differently
Trainee's perception of impractical training programs	Wanted practical tips but most of the information was theories.
Trainees' perception of irrelevant training content	What we learnt is what we learnt in college some of the new things are not applicable in our context.
Trainees' discomfort with change and associated effort	The traditional methods were more comfortable, easier and produced results.
Separation from inspiration or support of the trainer	Lack of confidence, there is a lot of risk in trying out the new approaches. Maybe training didn't provide enough practice
Trainees' perception of poorly designed/ delivered training.	The training was long with a lot of work. It should be called Diploma not certificate.
Pressure from peers to resist changes.	Why are you spending so much time on that (new approaches), can't you see how busy we are already?

Note. From Transfer *of Training. How to Help your staff Translate what they Learn into what they do.* July 04 2012, Griffith, G., & Allen, L.

It's important to understand the importance of school environment in the ELMT transfer in pre training self-efficacy and motivation as they have a significant influence in training (Latham, Millman, & Miedema, 1998;Tracey, Hinkin, Tannenbaum, & Mathieu, 2001). At this stage an individual's readiness to be developed contributes to his or her ability and motivation to learn. Hannah and Lester (2009) defined developmental readiness as the ability and motivation to attend to, make meaning of and appropriate new knowledge into one's long-term memory structures. In the change process foci it can be interpreted as the extent of the Headteachers wanting to change. According to Moss, Jensrud and Johansen (1992) regardless of how experienced the Headteachers were, they could still benefit from training and display improved leadership skills if steps were taken to enhance their developmental readiness. The development readiness promotes transfer of learning through the Headteachers' heightened realization of the existence of an important gap between the current status and the expected, aspired or ideal case. According to organizational learning theorists (Argyris, 1995; Senge, 1990), this shift in the mindset propels leaders to take action in acquiring new knowledge and implementing new behaviors, which in turn enable them to fulfill their leadership roles more adequately. If individuals are naively unaware of or actively resist the need for change, then attempts to get them to modify their behavior will be futile (Harris & Cole, 2007). Pre- training attitudes and mindsets will influence how the Headteachers took up the ELMT.

Post-training (workplace) environment appears to play a particularly important role; this research was being undertaken post-ELMT. For example, supervisory support for training and organizational support (in the form of formal policy and practices relating to the training) have been shown to influence transfer (Burke and Baldwin, 1999a). Workplace social and peer (coworker) support for the training can also influence transfer (Facteau, Dobbins, Russel, Ladd and Kudisch, 1995; Tracey, Tannenbaum and Kavanagh, 1995). As with any valuable learning endeavor, opportunities for constant review and re-working in the aftermath of training are required to ensure that learning is geared towards quality, relevance and sustained impact to the organization (Chin, 2011). In fact, the time allocated for participants to practice their new skills and knowledge seems to distinguish between programmes that merely teach about leadership and those that bring about true behavioral modifications (Moss et al, 1992). The length of the training and the structure was designed to allow a school term between modules. Liebermann and Hoffmann (2008) advice on the main goal of training designers should be to foster the trainee's motivation to use new skills on the job. This gave opportunities for the Headteachers to try out what they were learning. Through exploring the work environment, insights were drawn to understand how the teachers in the school supported the Headteachers in the transfer of ELMT skills.

Newstrom's (1986) identified the actions before, during and after training which will enhance the transfer of training of skills. The effect of actions at specific time was also supported by Saks and Belcourt (2006) "found that during training activities before, during and after training significantly added to the transfer of training" p. 14. It will be important to explore what was the perspective of the Headteachers to the activities listed by Newstrom's and understand the frequency of the implementation.

Chin (2011) poses a question from the change perspective; do leaders have the support and accountability to change? The research explored the post-ELMT support which contributes to this aspect, and took on three main forms: opportunities to demonstrate what has been learnt, organizational supportive structures (including direct manager guidance and monitoring), and peer support or networks (Chin, 2011). After the training, opportunities to practice the ELMT skills allowed Headteachers to display their new learning with more spontaneity and proficiency over time. The Headteachers were governing schools which were not-, low-resourced hence they needed to be skilled in opportunity identification.

Capitalizing on openings to transfer learning back to the school context could be a matter for leaders to identify situations for them where the new knowledge can be applied or could be explicitly catered for by a school which provides relevant developmental assignments and projects (Chin, 2011). However, since the conditions for real-life application are usually less propitious compared to the training environments, the quality of supportive structures within the schools also influences the success of behavioral change. Chin describes supportive structures as channels for obtaining feedback and guidance, such as coaching, mentoring, and "shadowing" or observing other more experienced leaders. These personalized development measures also subject leaders to some form of accountability for their own progress, and therefore heighten their commitment towards change. Finally, peer networks provide leaders with a supportive atmosphere that enhances their motivation for transferring learning, as well as the concrete assistance that they may require in making the transfer possible. Perceived peer support at work has also been shown to predict the amount of perceived opportunities to use new knowledge, skills and attitudes following training (Quinones et al., 1995). Exploration of the context and interaction will bring out the nature of support or networking expressed by the Headteachers. Newstrom (1986) identified Trainer, Trainee, Manager and organizations as

Table 4 *Dominant Sources of Transfer of training Barriers*

Trainee	Trainer	Manager	Organization	Barriers
2		1	2	Lack of reinforcement on the job
		2	1	Interference from immediate (work) environment
			1	Non supportive organizational culture
2***	1	2		Trainees' perception of impractical training programs
2***	1	2		Trainees' perception of irrelevant training content
1	2			Trainees' discomfort with change and associated effort
2**	2	1		Separation from inspiration or support of the trainer
2***	1	2	2	Trainees' perception of poorly designed/delivered training
		2	1	Pressure from peers to resist changes

Key: 1 = primary responsibility; 2 = secondary responsibility

Note * Organization in general means top management, the trainees' peer group and the physical factors in the work environment.

** Trainees may be a secondary barrier source if they are "seduced" into unquestioning acceptance of training content while in the presence of a skillful, expert inspirational trainer, only to discover the spell wears off upon returning to work.

*** Although these barriers may be perceptual, they are real to the trainees.

From "Leveraging Management Development through the Management of Transfer". By J. W. Newstrom, 1986, *Journal of Management Development, 5(5),* 33 - 45. dormant barriers to transferring ELMT tasks (Table 4). Bates (2003) recommend incorporating assessment of transfer from trainee, trainer and organization perspective as they will help create an environment that values and supports learning.

In this study the Headteachers (trainees), MoEST/TSC (managers) and organization (schools) will be the focus of analysis. Individual trainees' characteristics such as motivation and self-efficacy have been shown to have a significant influence on training transfer (Colquitt, LePine and Roe, 2000). In emphasizing the importance of individual characteristics (motivation to learn and apply), the work environment (supervisor support for learning and application), training design factors (identical elements-the similarity between the learning task and the application task), the profiling of the Headteachers and schools should be undertaken to a deeper understanding of the aspects (Baldwin & Ford, 1988).

Rouiller and Goldstein (1993) for example, identify organizational factors such as workplace cues (goal cues, task cues, social cues and self-control cues) and consequences (positive and negative feedback, punishment, no feedback) that are related to training. According to Rouiller and Goldstein, these cues and consequences guide individual learning and ELMT skills transfer, and therefore contribute to an organizational "climate" that can either inhibit or enhance learning and training transfer. Liebermann and Hoffmann (2008) appreciate the influence of the workplace as they observe that the archetype of any good workplace environment provides adequate resources and opportunities to apply the new knowledge. Organization systems have different levels that include the individual, the team and the organization which operate together as interacting subsystems within the overall organizational system (Kozlwoski and Salas, 1997). The review of the transfer of ELMT skills cannot be isolated to individual level but considered together has its importance to characterize contextual factors and processes that involve transfer of ELMT within the school. These contextual factors and processes can influence an individual's ELMT skills transfer through their perceptions of the organizational environment (Yamnill & McLean, 2001). However, the focus of organizational structure does not include social and cognitive process. Organizational structure may address policies and procedures; however transfer of ELMT may be influenced by lack of support from work teams or individuals (Pidd, 2002). The Headteachers cannot be evaluated alone but with the team and the structures they work with.

Successful transfer of ELMT skills will occur when behaviors and general concepts learned during training are retained and practiced in the workplace (Clarke, 2005), moreover, the transfer climate framework identifies contextual cues and consequences that can impact on transfer, but does not fully explain why cues and consequences may be inconsistent with each other in different contexts. An example of this is inconsistencies between school cues and consequences, and work group cues and consequences. Hence it was useful to analyze transfer of training from a perspective that builds on these two perspectives and offers a more comprehensive explanation of the social and cognitive processes that underlie transfer of ELMT skills.

Among the variables identified for focus of the research is the Headteacher, the manager (TSC and MoEST) and the school. School environmental factors that influenced transfer of ELMT were school commitment for ELMT, goals of the panels matched with new learning, climate of supportive and open communication, teachers have been valued, rewarded or given incentives for attending training, school hierarchy, and change-resistant climate (Hunter-Johnson, 2013). Alverez, Sala and Garofano (2004) identify organization as crucial influence to transfer especially where organization values learning as it will impact on employee performance. At the Headteachers' level, work environment factors that influenced transfer were discussion with supervisors to use new learning, supervisors' involvement or familiarization with the training, positive feedback from supervisor, opportunity to use new learning, positive feedback from co-workers, availability of tools, equipment or materials, pace of work flow, lack of mentor or role model, negative feedback from supervisor, lack of pace of work flow, availability of mentor role model, lack of tools, equipment, or materials, negative feedback from co-workers and lack of opportunity to use new learning (Hunter-Johnson, 2013). Van Den Bossche (2010) presents the influence of feedback to transfer of training with caution. According to Van den Bossche vigilance must be put in place when providing feedback, as feedback is not a panacea of improved behavior as popularly believed. With careful consideration of these factors, feedback can be used as an effective support mechanism to assist in the transfer of training.

Cromwell and Kolb (2004) studied the relationship between four work-environment factors (organization support, supervisor support, peer support, and participation) in a peer support network. Cromwell and Kolb revealed results that all four work environment factors have a statistically significant positive correlation with transfer. Velada et al., (2007) study revealed that transfer design, performance self-efficacy, retention of content, and work environment (feedback) were all significantly related to transfer of ELMT. However, supervisors' support did not significantly influence transfer of training. Headteachers are supervised by TSC and MoEST. Although the work of Velada et al., did not indicate a significant relationship between the supervisors and transfer of skills, the influence of quality assurance officers were explored to identify its impact for this context.

Business management aspects on transfer

The business management concepts are referred to as influencing the effectiveness of business. Some of these concepts could be transferred to school governance to demonstrate how the Headteachers could have handled transfer of training so as to have schools governed effectively and efficiently. A review of some business concepts explored how they could be linked to effective school governance and their possible influence on the transfer of ELMT skills for Headteachers who have attended ELMT

The transfer of ELMT skills will be influenced by how the Headteachers are able to identify hot spots in the school (Gratton, 2007). According to Gratton (2007) hot spot innovative capacity is linked to intelligence, insight and wisdom of working together with people. The success in transferring the ELMT skills will depend on the ability to identify the three aspects that influence hot spots, which include cooperative mind set, identifying boundaries spanners and sharing igniting purposes (Gratton, 2007). These aspects could be transferred to hot spots by changing the way they are structured, the standards they exposed and the conduct of the Headteachers.

Gratton (2007) advices in the reinforcement of five productive practices of appreciating latent making commitments, resolving conflicts, synchronizing time and setting a rhythm as a way of enhancing new approaches into practice. Gratton advice either tracking the hot spots for ignition, enhancement or sustainability (Gratton, 2007). The tracking will include locating hot spots, mapping systems, linking school goals, identifying potential leverage points and taking action. The applicability of these steps will depend on leverage based on identifying and analyzing the opposing and supporting forces through force field analysis (Nugent, 2002). These approaches would nurture new approaches to governance.

The implementation of new ideas means that there will be some teachers who will be working in an extra ordinary creative and collaborative way. The teachers will be working at different levels of enthusiasm and uptake of the new ideas. Transfer opportunities will be enhanced by supporting the first group so as to overcome the challenges of transfer of skills. The nurturing of the first group will depend on cooperative environment, which will influence the level and quality of interaction in a school hence guiding the establishment of hot spots (Gratton 2007). While handling the first group, the managers should be cognizant with the vital few. The identification of vital few and the others will enhance the Headteachers' understanding of their contribution towards the aspects in environmental models (Nugent, 2002).

On the contrary, caution should be taken to avoid over focusing on the few up-takers. It is important to balance between getting the good to better and great to terrific. Reh (2005) warns that the application of the principle is not the only focus but wisdom should also be included. The implementation of focusing on the vital few can be seen through different lenses in the ELMT skills transfer. The lenses include the analysis of the environmental model to identify resources and stakeholders roles. The implementation of the rule calls for broad implementation which is inclusive of success and challenges. Furthermore, the implementation needs a balance so as not to develop a blind spot among the trivial many or vital few depending on the situation.

Successful transfer of training could be enhanced by embracing Gratton's (2007) six practices of relation selection, induction, mentoring, collective rewards, peer working and social responsibility. The embracing of the practices has led to development of a cooperative environment. Gratton (2007) advices on the culture of employees, shaping the sharing of both implicit and explicit knowledge, therefore managers should identify sets of people who come with trust among themselves and allow them to work with each other and train the others. This offers opportunity to strategize so as to allow those who have taken up new ideas, to share with others in the school in a cooperative mindset environment.

During the transfer of ELMT skills there could be a possibility of a few teachers taking up the new approaches. There will be need to identify the few teachers in the school who would take up the new skills and therefore supporting them will empower them to influence the low/slow take ups. This will necessitate the types of boundaries within the school. Expansion beyond boundaries could be challenging due to economic environmental barriers. Hence, the Headteachers will need to explore capacities and interaction to create institutional values (Gratton, 2007). The exploration of common knowledge within the school will lead to continuous improvement; hence opportunities for social activities could inspire transcending boundaries. The teachers who are not up to task might be exhibiting latent energy (Gratton 2007). For this particular group the exploration ignition which may take three forms would offer some intervention (Gratton, 2007). Gratton explains that igniting question or igniting task to detect existing hot spots, big freeze and map the systems to try and understand why they exist. This information will help in harnessing potentially hot spots, as they continue implementing new ideas. There is a potential advantage in investing on people, time and money through force field analysis to nurture hot spots as they continue implementing new ideas (Nugent, 2002). The identification if quick and or high take up will offer strategic advantage in utilizing theme to prove the skills and influence the others in the school.

The transfer of ELMT skills will involve strategic planning. Whittington (2004) recommends that all strategies must include the processes and the desired outcomes. There is need to ensure the school is performing to cause the survival aspect of attracting parents and teachers, this would need the embracing of evolutionary approach to strategy (Gratton, 2007; White, 2004). As a response to economic environments the cultural context must be included so as to bring onboard many players with various opinions and approaches to strategy development (Hofstede, 1988). Strategic planning through environmental analysis will guarantee strategies mirroring the nature of the world in which the formulation is implemented (Nugent, 2002). The Headteachers' job demands the connection of processes and desired outcomes of strategies to ensure competitiveness (Whittington, 2004).

The skills that the Headteachers will be bringing to school are bound to impact on the competencies, hence the success of the school (White, 2004). This opens opportunities of establishing strategies that include the identification of competencies and ability to allocate the competencies where they will add value. The process of implementing the opportunities becomes more effective when the personnel involved are purposefully identified for value addition. Accurate identification and allocation require strategies that may involve reviewing performance, structures and processes.

Schools should be able to develop flexible structures, democratic change and new technologies. A strategic advantage involves combining emotional, social and intellectual capital as it develops a caring environment that allows people to reach out and work with others. Continuous effective interaction with people in the schools may offer success. A wide berth of options to the alternative strategies is provided by innovation, cost leadership and product differentiation which will generate competitive advantage when developed in consultation with the economic environment analysis (White, 2004). Each school has a school development plan towards the realization of its goal, hence the strategies, development of hotspots and performance management should be aligned to the vision of the school. For a strategist to achieve the mission and vision of a school there must be a strategic decision and strategic management. Hence, decisions in the school will be based on the ability to know the performance while the management will depend on structures that facilitate interaction and explore personal capacities.

When the Headteachers go back to the school, they will need to make multiple considerations. With multiple approaches to school governance, the need to be strategic and to implement most aspects becomes more crucial. One of the approaches recommended by White (2004) is environmental analysis to determine strategy and restrains. The environmental analysis should involve all the stakeholders and strategically inform the transfer of ELMT skills. The demands on the proposed approaches include risk analysis which is suggested by White (2004) to be incorporated as an aspect of strategic management. White's advice on basing strategies on SWOT (Nugent, 2002) to direct strategic plans is a potential aspect of addressing the multiple decisions making.

White (2004) recommends the approaches of strategies to be both conventional and distinct. While management identifies current educational trends and recommends training of the Headteachers. Scouting the ground was used to identify the contextual needs offers opportunity to begin transferring with contextual alignment. A methodological approach of transferring the ELMT skills would involve the management in the implementation of the skills bringing forth ideas that influence decisions. The approach nurtures strategies that are both conventional and distinct.

Gratton's (2007) ideas of innovation, exploration and exploitation would allow opportunities for interaction among cohort graduates across schools. The different contextual experiences would enrich the interaction making Gratton's idea of interacting with acquaintances, associates across boundaries practical so as to create innovative value as this diffuses information faster and creates value through energetic contribution and access to novel information. The interaction will be experiential learning offering insight in how to best deal with transfer challenges.

The application of Gratton's igniting questions may trigger curiosity and enthusiasm among the people involved. The application identifies existing hotspot and big freeze then maps systems to harmonize the potential hotspots. This provides opportunities to invest on people, time and money to nurture the emergence of the hotspot (Gratton, 2007). At the hotspots the people are at their comfort zone hence enhancing their productivity (Gratton, 2007). The approach identification and nurturing provides accommodation to the people preferences hence making them effective.

The tools for appraisal for growth instrument, monitoring, evaluation structure and analysis matrix for all the classes inform the progress of transfer in a timely manner. The three instruments address finance, participants, internal process and learning growth (Niven, 2002). The instruments offer an extensive view of all aspects, balancing focus including current and future performances (Stern Stewart Research, 1999). This allows the tracing of the the progress in transfer of ELMT skills. Effective development of the instruments is based on the vision of the school and the objectives are derived based on expected outputs. Systematic development of the tools includes the intention of the teachers ensuring it provides impact for transiting from implementing the tool to an operational one (Niven, 2002). The inclusion approach to the development of the tools impact on the effectiveness of the tools and the access and interpretation of the information derived from the tools.

Better understanding of the barriers to ELMT transfer of skills includes targeted implementation of the tools so as to articulate the causal effect (Dror, 2008; Niven, 2002). This allows the tools to measure the impact of the transfer of skills. However there is limitation due to the lag between cause and effect (Dror, 2008). The utility of these instruments should allow trading the success of transfer of skills, seeking more support by providing useful information. It will also provide information that will allow to the identification of processes that offer competitive advantage over the barriers.

There is difference between teams and groups for effective transfer of skills. Considering the schools' activities as projects because of the dynamics in the schools, where students are moving classes, and teachers are handling different sets of students at a given time offer opportunities to implement project management skills. This is similar to team dynamics and the role of mission and charter in project management. The project's mission and charter is the planning team's concise statement of core goals, values, and intent in order to provide the ultimate policy direction (Kerzner, 2009). The role of the mission and charter is to provide a powerful daily tool for judging the effectiveness in the transfer of ELMT skills. The acknowledgement of the distinction between a group and a team guides in the decision making as seen in Table 5.

The roles of a team include accomplishing known objectives especially on how an individual's role integrates the whole picture. This requires clearly defined roles, goals, vision and understanding individual responsibilities (Kaizenbach & Douglas, 1993). Lewis (1993) reinstates that the need to accomplishing goals, requires establishing and involving all from the beginning. The identification of the roles and how they will be implemented offer all the players guide on how to approach the transfer. According to Gist, Bavetta and Steven (1990) relevant goal setting will intensify the learner's interest in the tasks at hand which results in persistence from learners to reach the goal. Conversely, the creation of goals and vision require identifying each individual's perceptions of the team's goals, visions and establishing efforts, point of convergence hence increasing accommodation and collaboration.

Table 5 *Anne's definition of a group and a team*

Work group	Team
A group of individuals who generally work independently, coming together occasionally to discuss elements of projects but never really achieving the cohesiveness of a team.	A group of individuals who accomplish designated objectives by working interdependently, communicating effectively, and making decisions that impact their day-to-day work.

Note. From "Cross-functional teams in product development: Accommodating the structure to the process". D, Anne, (1993). *Journal of Productivity Innovation Management, 10*, 377-392.

There are opportunities of exploiting interdependence by appreciating diversity, talent complementality and valuing individual roles within the team while being cognisant of the opportunity and challenges offered. More respect for collective action on the part of team members, could lead to a perception of lack of independence on the part of his/her leader who is from a culture that respects individual action (Barczak, MeDonough, & Athanassiou, 2006). The uncertainty and possibility of failure is very much more proximal in the transfer of skills, than in general management. The interdependence versus dependence within the teams influences how the teams implement transfer.

Communication forms a formidable fabric in forming and sustaining a team. Open and honest communication will allow all the team members to be on the same page (Barczak, MeDonough & Athanassiou, 2006). This could be done through the following strategies for effective communication; frequent surveys to understand communication styles; paraphrasing to enhance active listening and finishing conversations with a question (Jungalwalla, 2000). Hayashi (2004) observes that better performance is based on sharing inside and outside knowledge in the group. On the contrary, in small doses conflicts have proved to be beneficial (Gobeli, Koenig, & Bechinger, 1998). To facilitate the development of social capital in the team's internal network, deliberate steps that include; providing time for team members to bond; identifying their mutual interests, needs; sharing information and encouraging collaboration on implementation and on problems critical for maintaining commitment and motivation should be taken (Barczak, MeDonough, & Athanassiou, 2006). Communication has a potential in influencing the transfer.

The type of teams affects the effectiveness of transfer. For instance, Anne (1993) views cross-functional teams as beneficial in supportive organizational structures and practices. However, Anne cautions that cross-functional teams cannot meet these measures on their own; nor be sustained in organizations that are "unfriendly" to the team concept. Cross-functional teams do not work reliably because the members feel stressed, neglected by the school and unsure of the rewards they will receive (Hong, Hahm, & Doll, 2004). One form of mitigation is developing cross-functional team's skills and experiences (Pons, 2008). The consideration of teams include the understanidng of the types of teams.

The urban setting provides teams that are often composed of individuals who are culturally, ethnically and functionally diverse (Grisham, 2010). Barczak, MeDonough and Athanassiou recommend initial identification of the particular qualities of a specific global team, such as mix(internal, external, across countries, cultures, languages, functions) and size, recognize and assess the team's characteristics, marshal appropriate managerial skills and personal attributes to manage team diversity right from the onset. This could turn the diversity to facilitate the transfer of skills than work against.

Leadership styles play different roles in implementing transfer of learning. The style of leadership needs to change as the transfer progresses (Lewis, Welsh, Dehler & Green, 2002). The task, goal, and demand dictate the type of leadership to be initiated. Investing in capacity building by developing social and academic capital for the teachers, panel heads and senior teachers in the school would facilitate the progressive leadership styles. The attributes of the leadership styles should correspond to strategic human resource management.

Robinson (2010) provides positive relational skills and interrelationships which include:-

- establishing and communicating learning goals and expectations.
- strategic resourcing allocated to prioritize transfer.
- direct involvement in planning, coordinating and evaluating the progress of transfer.
- promoting and participating in learning and developments.
- ensuring an orderly and supportive environment to facilitate focus on transfer of skills. While interaction is advocated by Gratton (2008) the inclusion of Robinson skills could enhance transfer.

Among the dimensions is the description of participative leadership in which the Headteachers have been associated with innovation success (Jeffrey, Michael & Shin, 2003). This dimension corresponds to Pons' (2008) required roles of managing a team namely by providing training and motivation, sorting out conflicts, appraising staff performance, and helping in decision-making.

As pedagogical leaders, Headteachers are faced with exploring ways of improvement. This includes exploring innovative ways and designing training for the implementation of the innovations. Stoll and Fink (1996) attribute to improvements which include sharing goals, responsibility for success, collegiality, continuous improvement, lifelong learning, risk taking, support, mutual respect, openness, celebration and humor. Most of the attributes reflect the characteristics of a team.

Soft management skills enable fairness and compassion among team members yet decisive in terms of attaining transfer of skill objectives, for effective leadership in all situations (Barczak, MeDonough & Athanassiou, 2006). However, the weaknesses though few, could have diverse impact towards management. The weaknesses should be addressed against their impact as they present a risk. Undertaking force field analysis frequently may facilitate effective transfer of skills to school governance (Nugent, 2008). The soft management skills will be informed by the outcome of the force field analysis.

Human resource is among the concepts of managing resources. Although the ELMT course covers the traditional approaches to HR, successful transfer of skills will be realized through innovation. Innovation provides leverage to HR roles leading to strategic advantages. Traditionally HR means monitoring terms and conditions of work through TSC, MoEST and KNUT then designing systems and practices that shape how people are treated in an organization based on a theory. The theories are guidelines offered by TSC, MoEST and KNUT on personnel management (Ulrich, 2008). According to Murray (2008) work trends are becoming unpredictable, varied and dynamic where the changing circumstances demand for new approaches to strategic public management. As the Headteachers are implementing the ELMT skills, the school governing approach will be changing. Hence, the innovation could shift the HR roles to a new approach of "HR management which includes decentralization, devolution and strategic planning" (Murray, p. 118). Headteachers are TSC agents; hence they play a key role as quality assurance officers. Through innovation the work trends will need to change according to Ulrich's ten aspects (Table 6).

Table 6 *Ten aspects and their innovative perspectives*

Aspect	Innovation Perspective
Change	Making sure that organizations change and adopt.
Communication	Learning to share information inside and outside the school
Execution	Making sure that strategies are delivered as planned.
Globalization	Adapting HR practices to a worldwide setting.
Governance	Building governance processes that ensure confidence.
HR infrastructure	Transforming HR function from traditional administrative service.
Intangibles	Identifying and delivering intangibles value to investors.
Leadership	Ensuring the next generation of leadership within a school.
Performance management	Desiring performance and results throughout the school.
Talent	Getting and keeping good talent.

Note. From *HR Dreams: Where Human Resource is Headed to Deliver Value.* D. Ulrich (2008). *Strategy, innovation and Change: Challenges in Management* by R. Galavan, J. Markides, & C. Murray, Oxford: OUP.

The innovative perspectives offer strategic approach to HR professionals in terms of designing, focusing their roles and those of their teachers. Ulrich proposes that the innovative perspective may lead to value creation. It demonstrates an open ended approach that is dynamic. The innovation could lead to the appreciation of teachers going for further studies, supporting them and placing them in roles of responsibilities which would utilize the skills earned. The innovation adds value to the school, buffers the quality of education and enhances the transfer of skills. The gain in leverage through system design leads to the prescribe value (Table 7)

Value creation requires mastering Ulrich's ten aspects and turning that knowledge into a set of organized capabilities. Murray (2008) warns that values are constantly in the making and demands that bedrock values should not be damaged. Although, the wide spectrum of the stakeholders might bring a challenge as it might be impossible to satisfy the whole group, taking leadership and ensuring most of the groups are satisfied with performance could overcome the challenge. Teachers can for instance be pushed to a point where they satisfy the stakeholders, despite feeling that their welfare is not being reciprocated. Value creation will mean broader sensitivity and tracking of performance in all sectors of the school.

Table 7 *Stakeholders and their prescribed values*

Stakeholders	Prescribed value
Teachers	Quality of contribution at work
Students	Satisfaction (value) from strategic service-High mean score, transition levels and quality of training
Donors-church / mosque/ government.	Level of institution sustainable performance
Management	Effectiveness of the tools and processes that ensure expressed strategies to happen

Manager's sensitivity and performance tracking brings up challenges on managing the value creation, opportunities to explore tools and techniques that will help overcome some of the challenges. Innovations demand for HR roles to respond in a way with aspects such as talent, shared mindset, and accountability, collaboration, learning generally and leadership. This can happen through appraisal system which could be used to track the implementation of the new ideas. Innovative, strategic clarity and efficiency added value to the school (Ulrich, 2008). Innovative HR roles identify the principles, that the HR are good at and exploring their capabilities to expand their abilities attracting dynamism. There is need to distinguish the two departments of HR roles. One department focuses on HR transaction, the other operates on transformation and strategic work (Ulrich, 2008). The two departments add value as transaction ensures efficiency, cost and error free work while transformation ensures strategies happen by accomplishing the ten aspects (Table 6). For sustainability, the innovation should go beyond splitting departments to offering currency on roles and delivering key aspects.

Furthermore, Headteachers should be aware of the five domains; personal credibility, knowing governance, mastering HR procedures, strategic contributions and learning to leverage HR technology (Ulrich, 2008). This awareness leads to competitive HR functions which are accurately structured.

Innovative HR roles include value addition and will demand the inclusion of coaching so as to align the leader's intent behavior as strategist. Ulrich (2008) identifies three dimensions to describe the change action, role and competencies. The combination of the three dimensions will determine the quality of the value addition. The role is seen as facilitation attuned to the change process and dynamic of large scale system change. Therefore, value addition makes the innovative HR professional coaches, architects, facilitators and deliverers, teacher's champions, administrative experts, strategic partners and change agents (Ulrich 2008).

The aspect of ELMT skills transfer to school governance can be equated to a project.

Staffing related factors describe the (mis)assignment of key personnel within the development process (Yazici, 2009). Smith and Reinertsen (1992) argue that it is important to assign capable (educated, experienced, tenured) members to transfer of skills in teams. The awareness of arguments touting the benefits of selecting team members with training and self-esteem, broad based competencies, high professionalism, and full time commitment should be beneficial (Burkat, 1994, Damanpour, 1991, Kerzner, 2009, Zhu & Heady, 1994). Insisting on the appropriate human resources provides success in the school's dynamic capability since human assets both individually and at the organizational level play a key role in success (Barney & Wright, 1988). Embracing the knowledge based view of the school, where the school's performance is related to its ability to create, transfer, and apply knowledge in an effective and efficient manner might support transfer (Spender & Grant, 1996). It is difficult to focus on a particular perspective and knowledge domain without acknowledging the influence of others (Cicmil, 2003). It is important to stimulate team learning and the exchange of knowledge at all levels of transfer and at all relevant levels of the departments/sections involved (Jorgensen & Emmitt, 2009). The handling of the transfer as a project would offer a competitive advantage.

Effective transfer of ELMT skills is interconnected, collaborative and involves context and content. Stacey (2003) urges the adoption of new methodologies of inquiry in studying the process of skills transfer. Knowledge is often assumed to exist independently of the context and the possibility of its capturing and codification is taken for granted (Cicmil, 2003). Conversely, power to create knowledge is not just with the Headteachers but also in the interaction with others and the environment. Therefore encouraging collaboration and strong communication among teaching team members will lead to better performance (Yazici, 2009). Knowledge and, learning are context dependent and are 'performed', actualized in conversations and other types of communication that involve individual and group relating in the medium of symbols, artifacts and power relations (Stacey, 2003). The very basic assumptions of school culture itself may restrain the knowledge – transfer processes (Eskerod and Skiriver, 2007). The levels of transfer will be influenced by interconnectivity, collaboration with the content and context.

The transfer of ELMT skills will have two approaches of project and process management. The application of Herzberg and Maslow's theories is important as the transfer of skills involves people undertaking tasks (Dartey-Baah & Amoako, 2011). The success of ELMT transfer of skills among other factors will depend on how the people involved in the ELMT skills transfer, experience satisfaction or dissatisfaction, are not dissatisfied or dissatisfied and their basic needs are either being met or not (Barczak, MeDonough, &Athanassiou, 2006). Gist et al. (1990) observe that the overall learner satisfaction is greater if the training is relevant to the job. According to Dartey-Baah and Amoako, statistically, money for teachers is not the best motivator instead, it's the interesting tasks that they work on, and of course respect. This concept is very important for teacher motivation (Barczak, McDonough, & Athanassiou, 2006). Monitoring, evaluation and review of the progress against the outcome will be crucial to the learning process and the success of future transfer. The involvement of both process and project management brings more players in the support of transfer.

The Headteachers will be undertaking an exercise of implementing new skills in environments they have worked in many years. School culture is a phenomenon which has an impact on implementing new skills (Belassi, Kondra and Tukel, 2007). Schein (1990) defines school culture as a pattern of basic assumptions that are invented, discovered or developed by the school community as they learn to cope with problems of external adaptation and internal integration that has worked well enough to be considered valid hence there is need to develop shared meanings, behaviors, and assumptions intended to produce successful school outcomes (Belassi et al., 2007). Implementing the ELMT skills is critical to the success of a school (Gresham, Hafer, & Markowski, 2006). Belassi et al. (2007) questions whether school cultures do support new product development programmes or whether there are systemic reasons that hinder their success. According to Belassi et al. transfer of skills structure may have little or no effect on transfer of ELMT skills to practice. Pfeiffer (1994) observes that traditionally envisioned sources of school success such as processes technology are less important than ensuring that an appropriate culture exists within a school. School culture is thus given prominence in the success of implementing ELMT skills.

Implementing ELMT skills are undertaken for different reasons and the appropriateness of a particular performance measure will depend on ELMT skills transfer strategy and objectives (Griffin & Page, 1996). Griffin and Page describe the success measures as trade-offs among several dimensions, hence for accuracy they use a multidimensional measure which offer a strategic approach.

Schools with strong top management leadership will tend to be more successful than their counterparts in transferring the ELMT skills (Belassi et al. 2007). The strength of the top management will be judged on how supportive they are on the transfer of skills. Belassi et al. advice that success comes by selling clear goals, encourage teachers to participate in decision making, delegate to teachers ways of achieving those goals, and encourage teachers to work on new ideas. Implementing ELMT skills primarily focuses on the effects of school-level variables such as transfer structure, ELMT skills transfer processes and how they are performed. The interaction between professional promotions and quality assurance and standards department has identified three dimensions namely the school's work environment, management leadership and school's results orientation (Belassi et al. 2007). Complete support of the top management and high demand on the follower to implement their skill will facilitate the transfer.

Entrepreneurial orientations (EO) are processes, structures and behaviors of schools that are characterized by five dimensions namely: autonomy, innovativeness, risk taking, proactiveness, and competitive aggressiveness (Lumpkin & Dess, 1996). The variation of the five dimensions interdependency have a possibility of posing a formidable challenge, when they manifest in ELMT skills transfer (Lumpkin & Dess, 2001). Exploring innovativeness as one of the EO aspects demonstrates school's tendencies to support fresh ideas and encourage creative processes in the direction of new approaches to school governance would offer support to transfer of skills (Gupta & Moesel, 2007). Innovativeness may bring up transfer issues because the whole school must buy the ideas. Most innovative ideas are clear to few people in the ELMT skills transfer and thus might bring tension.

However, risk-taking is also one of the worthy factors of EO. Kropp, Lindsay, and Shoham (2008) have defined risk-taking as being intended to do ambiguous practices, such as investing in unknown conflict between transactions and their uncertain results. Such approaches need clear commitment to the team, as to what it takes for the risk to bring results. The transfer of ELMT skills will have defined goals, timelines and the element of open risk-taking could be a challenge to the risk management aspects.

The transfer of skill will require proactiveness which is one of the dimensions of EO (Gurbuz & Aykol, 2009). Proactiveness refers to a predictive overview, which tends to take big steps on the path of exceeding challenges, gaining new opportunities and attending emerging work practices. Proactiveness can cause and distribute new opportunities; it can execute and exploit those opportunities to enhance information and meeting stakeholders needs (Nikoumaram & Heidarzadeh, 2006). Selecting which path to take will be a challenge to the Headteachers as they are guided by the ELMT skills transfer outcomes, while EO encourages competitiveness.

EO brings about trade-offs between building intra- and inter-industry socialites quite differently. EO develops new routines, competencies, and technologies and therefore need networks rich in bridging ties for new combinations of productive factors (Low & Abrahamson, 1997). Competitiveness and aggressiveness may be a challenge in harmonizing the teams involved in the transfer of skills.

Headteachers get back to school as individuals; hence autonomy which refers to the independent action of an individual or a team, in bringing forth an idea or a vision and carrying it through to completion is a crucial aspect to consider. According to Kanter (1983), it requires the exercise of autonomy by strong leaders, unfettered teams or creative individuals who are disengaged from school constraints, to lead in EO environments. The Headteachers will have a daunting task to balance autonomy and task management.

School culture (SC) has a strong basis of team's intra- and inter-industry social capital. EO influences the configuration of the team impact on SC (Stam & Elfring, 2008). Entrepreneurship brings on board, the five dimensions which formulate the EO. The human capital of the team members should evaluate of the member's social capital, during the process of team norming, forming, storming and performing (Stam & Elfring, 2008). The evaluation brings out the understanding of the stages of the team as well as the capacity for support by the individual members.

Measurable variables are easy to manage, because of their quantifiable nature hence they can easily be linked to motivation. The design of compensation structure and how it promotes desirable teachers' behavior is instrumental to successful transfer of skills. Innovation will improve school governance based on novel ideas (Burbiel, 2009). Based on the technical information, a school has many attributes to consider, such as relative advantage, compatibility, complexity, trial ability, cost and community approval in support of transfer of ELMT skills. Compensation and innovation could manage the variables in a way that supports transfer.

As Headteachers transfer their skills, it will call for teachers to work differently. This calls for negotiation to convince the teachers to do it, making it comprehensive on the outcome (Readon & McLaughlin, 2008). Technology such as skype and video can support the innovation through remote interactions with other schools or Headteachers. The connectivity offers opportunities of virtual learning through accessing successful models of tranfer of skills.

The ability to influence organizational norms, conduct influenced decisions, determine the level of quality communication, buy-in and cooperation provides a competitive advantage on transfer of skills (Nada, Andrew, & Lee-Davies, 2008). Communication challenges are managed, by selling the ideas according to teachers' terms. According to Readon and McLaughlin (2008) stakeholder's terms mean their interest, desires, deep-seated beliefs, and likely action. Readon & McLaughlin argue that, information is changing at a very high rate hence we should be "more focused on updating and plausability of the information and less on forecasting and acccuracy" (p. 284). The access to information and how it is handled offers insights on the levels of transfer and potential actions for improvement.

Information technology (IT) could enhance individual and school learning. School learning is an aspect of system thinking, which may be achieved through insight. Senge (1990) suggests that to gain insight, various mental models must be used to interpret perception and information. According to Senge, school learning is influenced by gaining insight both inside and outside the school. ELMT skills enables the Headteachers to access, explore opportunities of information through connectivity. Utility of IT will facilitate gaining insight, both internally and externally hence facilitating school learning. Since individual and school learning is influenced by the access of information, the Headteacher's exploitation of IT offers a pillar that may facilitate learning depending on how it supports the access. IT offers information glut hence the ability to sift and search for appropriate information as per the needs would address the transfer.

The growth of a school is based on its learning ability (Honey & Culp, 2005). According to Honey and Culp, the learning ability is influenced by the logistics capability of the school to link different aspects of the school. The linkage is offered by the connectivity facilitated by IT. Having gone through ELMT, Headteachers have been empowered with IT skills, as part of their training. According to Cho, Ozment, and Sink (2008) learning orientation could be linked to the school performance. The internet provides a dynamic medium for channeling information between schools (Banduchi, 2005). IT includes internet connections and software which can provide data and voice between the school and other sources (KICD, TSC). The transfer of skills could be enhanced through utilizing the resources provided by the government and other educational partners. The role of IT is therefore important in the information flow, organization and storage. In their research in two countries Hwang, Jung, and Salvendy (2006) established that majority of both country's subjects in their research used the internet almost every day for learning among other uses.

There is a dual relationship between learning in schools and distribution of infrastructure. The success of the Headteachers' transfer of skills will be delivered by how well they develop the structures. The nature of the structure could influence behavior impacting on the way of thinking of the school. Furthermore, school learning could influence the design of the structure to strengthen learning. The Headteachers will be bringing on board new information and structure to improve school governance. The structure will determine the organization of the information hence having impact on the relevancy and timelines of the information accessed. Relevancy and timelines will determine the effectiveness of the individual on school learning. Strategic use of IT provides relevant information to appropriate individuals or team depending on the needs at specific times (Tsai & Hung, 2008). The interrelationship between learning, IT and teaching could facilitate interdependence which may be an indicator that individuals or school learning could be influenced by IT structures.

Learning is the process of acquiring information, reflecting on the information and making meaning from it. IT utility in school governance will facilitate the acquisition and spreading of information (Hirose and Sonehara, 2008). Hence for the individual, it offers aspects of self-growth through the learning opportunities while for the team it will be learning among individuals for collective development. IT could facilitate, enhance and extend what was offered during ELMT. Senge (1990) outlined five disciplines that can help a school and its individuals improve their effectiveness within the ever-changing school environment. His position was that systems' thinking is the glue that binds and integrates the other four disciplines. System thinking, facilitated by IT to involve interrelationship and connectivity aspects which include, knowing what other parts of the subject panels are doing and making a decision to complement their activities. Senge's disciplines can be applied with the use of IT to improve organizational effectiveness by supporting its organizational knowledge building and its utilization.

The utility of IT could enable scenarios to be captured and stored or simulated based on the data collected. IT can be used to retrieve and create scenarios to offer individual learning opportunities to see how the implementations of the new skills are impacting the school. Databases will enable information access and recreation of scenarios when need arises. This will help in learning, sharing the impact and influencing more teachers in the school.

Simultaneously there is an advantage or a possible danger depending on the type of information being shared (Hirose & Sonehara, 2008). The danger could be posed when irrelevant information such as rumors is circulated by IT (Ito & Kagaya, 2006). The type of information and the nature of the individual receiving it might cause a mismatch causing a misunderstanding (Hirose & Sonehara, 2008). This is further complicated by the fact that the need to transfer knowledge varies with communication (Walsham, 2002) . Managing information system ensures that the systems respond to the needs of the school. Senge (1990) calls for the development of self-discipline to help people accomplish this through the personal mastery approach.

Strategic use of IT offers learning opportunities to both individuals and organizations. The Headteachers will need to be aware that the choice of information and how it is utilized may develop a team. Both the individuals and the team have an opportunity to learn at their levels (Nonane & Tekeuchi, 1995). A team refers to the interrelationships between individuals or sections. The complimentary association among these units is what makes the team. The commonality between sections or individuals will become a team when they are linked through eLearning. Because of their shared vision and the fact that the individuals will be seeking to achieve a similar goal the convergence of their operation will initiate connectivity.

A group of Headteachers working will be individually trying an intervention on improving the school governance by introducing new pedagogies. With the provision of laptops to schools and the one laptop per child training to headteachers, the infrastructure and access to technology has changed. This has also influenced many PLS to include ICT enhanced pedagogical leadership training (Gioko, 2013). From this training online professional leanring are opportunities exposed to the headtecahers. The Headtecahers therefore seek professional assistance from a variety of online facilities. Each Headteacher may not know what the others are doing but has an inherent shared goal. When the Headteachers will start to register in some sites they will begin to see each other online. If they start to monitor what others are doing in different schools, this will later become a working group undertaking an intervention with the same goal. This was actually evident when the Headteachers were doing a blended learning through KEMI for another related PLS. The creation of this team could be facilitated by IT. IT will facilitate the connectivity between schools and make them formulate a team for effective intervention activities.

Schools as institutions have many services to offer. The Headteachers who have undergone ELMT training have gone through managing resources; schools will not have the expertise to do all the services they will need to embrace outsourcing. The global changes demand effectiveness in management, which calls for a dedicated focus to strategic issues. Among the observed trends is management engaging expertise from profit seeking specialists who enjoy enormous economies of scale. For example printing of end of a school term or monthly tests a photocopy company can supply photocopies and manage them in a school instead of the school buying their own.

IT outsourcing will be beneficial to the school. First the focus of outsourcing has moved from cost saving to enhancing strategies capabilities (Glassman, 2000). Glassman (2000) argues that the opportunities are attributed to either the outsourced firm specializing or having a probability of innovation or more time allocated to key issues, because the vendor is running other issues. According to Glassman, a specialist is able to mobilize quality diverse capabilities to provide technical solutions leaving Headteachers to exploit the benefits offered by focus and specialization. Specialists are experts hence they bring on board specific experiences that will benefit institutions.

Secondly, Levina and Ross (2003) and DiRomualdo and Gurbaxani (1998) cited in Qu, Pinsonneault and Oh (2011) found that IT outsourcing can provide schools with various economic, technological and strategic benefits such as reducing IT operation costs, improving technical competence, and even providing firms with competitive advantages. Cost reduction is an aspect of adding value to the school while technical competence will raise the school's profile. The two aspects will favorably place the school on the competitive map.

Third, Glassman (2000) asserts that outsourcing non-strategic processes eliminates a distraction enabling the managers in this case Headteachers to focus its distinct capabilities on areas critical to its strategic success (teaching, learning and assessment). Allocating specific roles to specialists and leaving the Headteachers with crucial roles is bound to impact on the effectiveness of the ELMT skills transfer.

Fourth, Loh and Venkatraman (1992) argue that the cost of IT governance has direct impact on the cost effectiveness of running the school. Under such an argument it is indicative that the adoption of IT outsourcing will be a conscious effort for the school to enhance its ability to create value for its stakeholders. And fifth, Aucoin (1991) considers outsourcing as an attractive option because it allows schools to streamline their internal cost structure while obtaining critical technological capabilities.

Headteachers' decisions are judged by the effect they have on the school's FPE budget. Glassman (2000) observes that IT has been found as one potential area of outsourcing. This could be attributed to the outsourcing firms, taking a short time to absorb multiple IT aspects in a school. Loh and Vinkatraman (1992) contend that firms that outsource have generally performed substantial benefit-cost analysis, and expect that the change in IT governance will be perceived favorably by the stakeholders. The emerging trends have seen institutions engaging in IT outsourcing with mixed outcomes.

Hayek (1937) observes that change has a possibility of leading to implications that economic theories aren't important which is problematic. According to Hayek, continuous flow of practice is maintained by constant deliberate adjustments. The circumstances of time and place should be incorporated during planning. Based on such background, Headteachers familiar with knowledge of relevant changes and resources play a key role in facilitating authentic decisions. It is crucial to track the changes happening and include them in the decisions made. Hence resource utilization should not only be considered through source and recipient but also on the nature of the source and the recipient. Knowledge acquisition and common communication cannot be determined by a single observer, it must be cognizant of imperfection in human knowledge.

Drucker (1995) observes that development has brought up tools which can be used in governance. However, the tools are either understated or unused. The observation is true because progression in advancement has outpaced the human rate of adoption. Most tools are either underutilized or ignored due to lack of skills and knowledge, ignorance and the comfort of the current practices. Such scenarios are Headteachers graduating with ELMT skills and going back to school. There are many systems Headteachers could use to govern schools. Drucker (1995) presents such tools as traditional and activity costing. He outlines traditional as focusing on task only, while activity is all inclusive. The inclusiveness of the later approach provides cost information and yields control. The knowledge of such information will enable Headteachers to make decisions on which type of costing to use, to realize effectiveness. Knowing about cost alone will not be successful as the knowledge of the entire financial chain will enable the management of costs and minimization of yield (Drucker, 1995). Costing in isolation will not yield much and needs to be integrated in the entire economic chain.

In reality, even with the same school uniformity is non-existent because each department believes their option as the only possible or better option (Drucker, 1995). Drucker offers some hope by presenting some schools which have tried to overcome the challenges by finding ways to avoid the increasing cost disadvantage. The documentation of success stories offer possibility of sharing and influencing more people. Access to such knowledge might have an impact on the adoption.

Access to information enables making informed judgment. The diagnostic tools include foundation-, productivity-, competence- information and information about the allocation of scarce resources (Drucker, 1995). These tools are to be used complimentarily because they inform and direct tactics. Through ELMT the Headteachers are exposed to strategic planning where they will require Political Environmental Social Technological Educational hence the knowledge on environment and technology is crucial.

Governance failures are brought about by the assumption that aspects must be what we think they are or should be. Decision making needs continued access to the information required and the type of information must be known to the Headteachers. Technology will enhance the possibility of activity based costing but the focus should not only be on the tool but on the concept behind it. Drucker (1995) identifies the new approach of information as a base for "future action rather than a postmortem or a record of what has happened" p. 62.

Access to knowledge is an aspect that could be empowering. It is crucial for Headteachers to understand the type of knowledge they are seeking as well as where the knowledge exists and how to access it. Moreover the access to the knowledge does not prove to be effective unless the knowledge is utilized well. On the other hand, knowledge can be discouraging when different aspects of the knowledge are not pieced together to complement each other or some aspect of knowledge which are complimenting are ignored due to reference of certain schema. The ability to understand both aspects of knowledge will influence choices made in seeking the knowledge and the level of implementation. The awareness of all these elements of knowledge would facilitate modeling which will enable teachers to take it up beyond access. The role and status of the knowledge recipient and source are also crucial to determine the effectiveness of the access. However, the role, status and access need to be in tandem to determine the knowledge to be accessed and its impact.

Teachers have long been recognized as school's stakeholders (Van Buren H. J., 2003). Teachers can be identified as moral claimant stakeholders (Kaler, 2002) to whom the school has morally obligatory perfect duties (Kaler, 2003). The level of involvement and commitment in teacher's practices has effects for Headteachers and teachers (Appelbaum, 2000). Relationships with teachers should be explored in the consideration of the potential of the parents, Headteachers and teachers.

Teachers and Headteachers engage with each other due to the nature of their profession. Teachers prefer a more stable employment even if they feel that they earn less than they deserve (Freeman & Rogers, 1999). The continued employment is a matter of choice (Narveson, 2003). Nerveson further links such an engagement as the teacher offering their service at a price offered by the TSC. However the headteachers feel as if they are helping the teachers on one have while the teachers feel as if they are helping the Headteachers on the other hand. The relationship presents a mismatch (Van Buren & Greenwood, 2008). In reality Headteachers have a notion that they are helping the teachers, while the Headteachers feel that they are being helped by the teachers. Such notions encourage unethical acts which erode the relationships between teachers and Headteachers. Such a mis-match in employment relationship could encourage unethical acts which might erode the relationship between the Headteachers and the teachers.

Teachers must be provided with comprehensive information in a timely manner. Headteachers Stipulating clear working rules and agreement on the rules by the teachers avoids issues of exploitation (Narveson, 2003). Furthermore, Nerveson notes that exploitation may be observed, for instance when a Headteacher grows in the job earning a large pay, while a younger teacher earns less despite working more. While the reasons teachers contribute to the school may vary. All teachers seek benefits, and protection from harm hence information and agreement is crucial

Headteachers getting back to school would expect all the teachers to embrace the new skills and implement them as shared by the Headteachers. Employees have a preference of being treated equally irrespective of any aspect that has nothing to do with ability (Abella, 1985). According to Abella, individuals should be given an opportunity to use their abilities according to their potential and not according to expectations. Hence as the Headteachers demand the embracing of the new skills they should appreciate the diversity in competencies and differentiate the. demands according to competencies (Narveson, 2003). By allocating tasks based on potential, The Headteachers will be creating an inclusive working environment which will influence the rate of skill transfer.

ELMT encourages the Headteachers to network with stakeholders. The stakeholders include the community in which the school is situated hence; a school exists within a society as a third party (Nerveson, 2003). The society is made up of many aspects, including people's status, culture and environment. Activities for public good and aligned to the community will not cause harm, conflict or discontent (Narveson, 2003). In fact schools become refuge centres during strifes or calamity; hence, they are looked upon by the community.

Schools should have policies that safeguard the availability of finite resources for the future generations (Narveson, 2003). The ELMT skills gained by the Headteachers ensure that they supplement the social structure and not go against it. However, there are some issues that might bring tension, for example a community that believes in early marriages and no schooling for girl child will be against the ELMT advocacy of equitable access to school by all children. Being sensitive and creative in creating awareness and influencing the community without tension will attract community support to transfer.

Engagement with the school community should not cause harm or deception to the teacher involved. The engagement should be based on mutual benefit for those involved and should not be based on nepotism, tribalism or exploitation (Narveson, 2003). The school policies should look at these aspects to have an accommodating working environment beneficial to the school. There should be clear policies which guide the school to realize their goals, without harm while being aligned to government policies.

With the FPE, the Headteachers have become accounting managers. This calls for embracing accounting skills to respond to the needs of the schools. The ELMT offers a session which exposes the Headteachers to accounting skills. To enhance their management skills, the Headteachers need to understand the inaccuracies in the current accounting systems, and explore opportunities for involving their teachers. According to Stewart (2002) books do not represent the actual situation but rather the required states. The FPE funds being managed by the headteachers have brought out issues of fraud and incompetency's on financial management. On the other hand the books are utilized specifically by different stakeholders. The Headteachers need to realize that the multiplicity of representation leads to lack of reality hence it impacts on decision making especially on the doctored reports.

It is erroneous to associate financial sources and investment uses (Stewart, 2002). Stewart outlines that "failure to align [the] accounting principle to economic values has forced managers to live in two worlds" (p. 6). The dual situation is very dicey as single decisions cannot be sustained in twin forked conditions. The economic measures as suggested by Stewart will be the best approach because they are stable. The best approach is the economic measures which are stable and have a positive effect on stakeholders.

Associating finance sources with investment has been identified as erroneous. Stewart (2002) observes that "debt exaggerates the apparent payoff which a school earns from its investments" (p. 5). Stewart warns that that Headteachers might be tempted, while handling bad debts to provide a cushion for lean times. The provision of the bad debt reserve, does not provide accurate information because the bad debts are estimates in the event of payment, the money could be used for "smoothing reported earnings and stabilizing bonuses" (Stewart, p. 17). The prediction of bad debt is usually a probability and it is important for the Headteachers to take precaution and put up intervention measures as they have done currently. However what they do with the payment needs to be tracked so that risks are contained. A key issue on loans is the pre-booked losses vs. pre-recorded grossed up interest on paid loans, Stewart (2002). According to Stewart the accountants usually prefer the latter because of the benefit of doubt. The benefit of doubt is biased as it only considers one side.

Headteachers should be aware that intangibles are not recognized as realistic assets by the current practice yet they are important in spearheading development and new products. On the contrary professional development is not handled as an asset but as a cost (Stewart, 2002). Stewart advices the importance of capitalizing investments because of a knowledge based economy. Headteachers should appreciate that professional learning opportunities and research should be seen as assets because they act as seeds which impact on the growth of the schools.

Stewart (2002) observes that full cost accounting is not being implemented as only successes are recorded, yet in a probability situation the non-occurrences chances ought to be considered as well because "failure of something is knowledge and knowledge is capital in an intangible economy" (p. 17). Headteachers need to offer holistic presentation because it is important to be inclusive and point out the losses too.

Strategic investments take time to bear fruit, hence "measuring [economic value added] EVA without an adjustment will lead to dramatic understatement of performance in the initial building years and an overstatement in the lush later years" (Stewart, 2002, p. 22). Headteachers should appreciate that it is very important to make informed and matching adjustments that will allow accurate measurement of EVA at all times.

The inclusion of teachers in decision making has its potential gains to the school. According to Schönburg & Stern (1999), EVA will allow a school to give decision rights and incentives to teachers, they advise with proper implementation of the EVA, there is gain to the teacher "without loss to Headteachers" (p. 3). However, it could offer challenges due to teacher's ability to make decisions. It could be argued that teachers need information to know what is happening in the school. On the other hand, decision making requires access of information from multiple sectors. Headteachers should be cautious as they involve teachers noting that decision making with a large number of teachers at different levels might be challenging and inefficient.

Schönburg & Stern (1999) links teacher's productivity and sharing of best practices with creation of potential value enhancement. EVA charges for all factors of productivity. Schönburg & Stern suggest that "continuous improvement in EVA always furnishes stakeholders with an increase in value" (p. 4). Teachers play a crucial role in the productivity of the school. As Headteachers transfer their ELMT skills to school governance, they should appreciate the potential of teacher's involvement.

A complimentary role is represented by Hayek (1991) as cited in Schönburg & Stern (1999) who sees the inclusion of the teachers as allowing the decision to source information from all sectors. However, it could be argued that the access of information by the Headteachers and the teachers is not at the same depth and breadth. Unless the whole group is able to possess similar access and interpretation, inclusion might be reduced to a complementary role.

Shiely's study found out that performance metric has to be two things, it has to be understandable and it has to be well linked to value (Schönburg & Stern, 1999). A review of teachers involvement revealed that the "participation caused greater productivity levels in all cases" (Schönburg & Stern, 1999, p.7). However with success "the total number of [teachers] participation in the financial results of their enterprises is still quite small" (Schönburg & Stern, p.7). On a positive note, different sectors are advocating for teacher's participation. Unions have come into play to support the teachers' financial participation. They have advocated for a regional collective bargain, a move which has been opposed by teachers who prefer negotiations at school levels. Headteachers should embrace participation as the empowered teachers will then support their approvals to governance.

Case studies by Trade union Congress (TUC) partnerships to deliver "change management, communication, the development and mobilization of in-house talent, the dissemination of best (teaching) practice, and improves the performance of the personnel function" (Schönburg & Stern, 1999, p. 11) could offer strategies to enhance transfer. Through case studies the Headteachers will be able to trace the progress in ELMT skills transfer.

Managers must be wary of the challenges of involving employees, yet it adds value and increases productivity. Schönburg & Stern (1999) identified a few challenges such as manager's delegate very little to their subordinates, demonstration of ignorance or lack of interest and accounting standards therefore, "mangers require a common framework, a common language, and a similar set of tools in order to evaluate choices and discern the right decisions" (p. 10). Inclusion and delegation broadens the people who will be involved in the transfer.

Performance management is a skill offered in the ELMT, which is new to the Headteachers. According to the TSC, performance contracts have been introduced in schools, hence Headteachers will be able to bridge the transfer gap if they are able to understand Activity Based Costing (ABC), the Balanced Scorecard (BSC) and Economic Value Added (EVA) which are modern tools for performance measurements and management (Schinder & McDowell, 1999). The decision on which tool(s) to use depends on the knowledge of whether the tools are mutually exclusive or can be used together. Factors should according to Dror (2008), be considered when analyzing organizational performance management tools. EVA provisions could influence the preferences of its utility. EVA provides practical applications which can be embraced. EVA provides information that will allow decisions made by the Headteachers to be aligned with school goals (Brewster & Chandra, 1999). Therefore, it facilitates the managers' performance evaluation and compensation. EVA provides a common language across the school, which reduces confusion compared to using the other systems. Commonality allows the use of a single matrix in a variety of management processes. The use of a common measurement allows accountability as well as simplicity. Schönburg and Stern (1999) observe that "managers and employees require a common framework. . . language, and... tools in order to evaluate choices and discern the right decisions" (p. 10). The provision of EVA which includes information and common language responds to the requirement of managing for value.

Current trends and competition have pressured Headteachers to deliver value, deriving more accurate and transparent performance measurement. The drive to seek alternative modes of performance and management tracking is based on competition (Schinder & McDowell, 1999). Alternatives bring out the challenge of making preferences on which alternative(s) to select. Among the frameworks ABC, BSC and EVA to be analyzed, the focus is on making preferences on how to handle these frameworks either simultaneously or mutually exclusively (Schinder & McDowell, 1999). The analysis of each framework according to Utley's (1999) cited in Dror (2008) suggestions, offer informed choices on making preferences to cope with the current trends and competition hence delivering value.

The characteristics of BSC influence its preference over other frameworks. BSC is extensive and includes a broader view of the aspects captured (Schinder & McDowell, 1999). Dror (2008) identifies BSC as a fundamentally strategic framework for individual schools. According to Norton and Kaplan the designers of BSC are meant to translate the school vision and strategy into objectives. The operationalization of the school vision into objectives strategically aligns the school goals to the vision. The extensive nature of the BSC allows for multiple aspects to be included in performance management. Effective performance requires a holistic outlook of all the aspects so that rewards or decisions are adequately made. BSC allows for the collection of data that helps to balance focus between current and future performances (Schinder & McDowell, 1999). However Dror (2008) notes that BSC does not consider time lag between cause and effect. Performance management requires the inclusion of time because some ideas require incubation for benefits to be seen. BSC limits the performance evaluation within a financial period, hence being exclusive. It also provides room for manipulation.

The success of BSC is based on its activity to raise awareness. BSC advantages include sequential objectives, capability to support long term programs, potential to select relevant performance and measures based on real dates and two feedback levels (Dror, 2008). On the contrary, the potential could be challenged. As Dror (2008) argues, BSC lacks basic guidelines for selecting performance measures and it has no method for selecting targets to measure. BSC is flexible, however flexibility demands that the scorecard measures can only be determined after the overall strategy is understood. This will imply that a goal which summarizes the interaction between variables has been identified (Schinder and McDowell, 1999). Responses to challenges will be the management's task, however bottom-line. The shareholders/ stakeholders concern is earning adequate return on investment.

BSC focuses on learning as the only source of causality (Dror, 2008). As performances on the variable are tracked, it is important to measure accountability. Success indicators should be easily understood and identified from the variables independently without making interaction between the variables. On the other hand, simplicity should be advocated so that the information got can be adequately used in decision making. It should be important to build and maintain relevance of the defined measures to benchmark performance. Fluidity in the measurement standards will not provide continuity in decision making. Causality based learning is dynamic and can be stage managed. The learning offered by BSC should only be authentic if it goes beyond causality. Understanding the limitations and exploring how they can be addressed will influence the decision of making BSC a preference.

The analysis of the framework is one aspect of informing decision to make preference. There are other critical issues such as motivation, simplicity and commitment suggested by Schinder and McDowell (1999) which must be looked at when selecting a framework. Schinder and McDowell warn that the volume of information will not necessarily lead to better decision; hence there must be motivation to act upon new information. They advocate on a balance between simplicity and accuracy. The success of a framework will depend on the right decisions being made from the new information, derived by the framework (Schinder & McDowell, 1999). The uptake of a framework will depend on how easy it is to understand it. However, simplicity should be guided to maintain a credible state of providing the appropriate information for strategic decisions. Schinder and McDowell (1999) also identify commitment as a critical element because the adoption of a framework depends on the level of commitment. Moreover, success will also depend on the impact of Headteachers' behavior because teachers add value to the school which is a derivative of performance management. Schinder and McDowell assert that the sustainability of a successful organization is based on the culture of value creation. Schinder and McDowell warn that "the use of management system alone [will] not create sustainable change" (p. 5). Hence there should be a link connecting the whole system of decision making, performance evaluation and compensation.

Motivation, simplicity and commitment will influence the understanding of the preferred framework and its successful implementation.

The complementarity of the frameworks calls for an integrated approach, because they require information, decision frameworks, performance measures and rewards to perform. Good strategies, cannot work without understanding the framework, and being motivated and committed to execute the strategies and produce results. However, the motivation will be derived from the development of a working knowledge of the tools, hence a call for simplicity. Effective decisions cannot be made from piecemeal information but through a holistic approach. This demands an integrated approach which explores the complementarities of each tool, so as to overcome their limitation and offer complementing information. The aspects of the complementarities are combined to give a holistic picture. The key is balancing capital and costing, simplifying the frameworks, being motivated and committed and understanding the tools.

Summary

The review of literature focused on the transfer of skills after a period of training, barriers to transfer of skills, the ranking of the barriers, and the actions of the CP's and the impact of the barriers before, during and after the training and the business management skills applicable in managing or overcoming the barriers to the transfer of training.

The literature stipulates that there are factors that the Headteachers explored for them to decide what to implement from the dearth of information that they received in ELMT. It was also noted that the transfer of skills was a continuous process after the training. The time after training was seen as a factor with various researchers giving different percentages of what is applied and the failures and investment results. Several barriers have been identified as being the barriers to transfer of skills. The barriers have been ranked with the greatest referring the leadership theoretical views and the least referring to leadership philosophy endorsed by the organization. The barriers to training have different impact at different times, before, during and after the training. Several aspects have been given by research to explain how the impact of the barriers varies at different timelines. Dominant sources of the transfer of training barriers have been identified in the CP, trainer, manager and the organization. This brought to fore the exploration of the individual characteristics and organization factors and their role on the transfer of skills. Selected business management concepts have been reviewed as present to offer a possible solution to overcoming the barriers to transfer of skills. Hotspots have been identified as an approach that can be used to nurture the people supporting the transfer of skills.

Focusing on the vital few presented an aspect that can ensure that the focus is on the trivial many and the vital few in case of successes and converse in case of challenges to transfer of skills. Aspects of strategic planning have been explored indicating that the Headteachers could be empowered by the approach by offering a competitive advantage. The concepts of teams have established how they can be handled to enable the Headteacher succeed in the transfer of skills. The leadership styles have been found to be varying as the Headteachers transfer their skills, it has been seen that tasks and people will influence the type of leadership enabling the transfer of skills. The management skills have also been found to play a role where advanced strategic management will be instrumental. The management is both of resources including human resource.

The review indicates that the Headteachers should take HR roles leading to strategic advantages. Performance tracking, value creation and value addition have been identified as playing a key role in strategic management. The management of resources could be enhanced through outsourcing services allowing the Headteachers to focus on their core business. The transfer of skills can be equated to a project, hence project and processes management have been identified to play a role in enabling the transfer of skills. EO has also been established to provide dimensions that will offer a platform to address the barriers. EO does not stand alone as it influences the configuration of teams hence shaping SC. Technology advancement has offered opportunities which could be explored to address the barriers presented. Technology could facilitate information access and networking among other things, and could be used to improve organizational effectiveness. Stakeholder's engagement has been explored to bring to fore their level of participation, support and how they could play a key role to the success of the transfer of skills.

FPE means the Headteachers have become financial managers as they handle the FPE money in schools. The integration of advanced accounting systems including EVA will place the Headteachers at an advantageous position of overcoming the barriers. The take up of performance management will see them embracing ABC, BSC and EVA as organization performance management tools. The complementarity of the frameworks will empower the Headteachers to overcome some of the barriers.

The aim was to find out to what extend the exposed skills were into practice, the barriers they faced and how they were overcome the barriers. The review of literature brought to fore, the business management aspects and how they could be used to enhance the transfer of ELMT skills to school governance. These aspects were reviewed in light of how the Headteachers could manage the barriers. The outcome on the level of implementation of the business management skills will inform the recommendations for effective ELMT skills transfer to school governance.

Chapter 3: Methodology

This chapter explains the research design, describing the methodology and the rationale for the approach. The chapter further explains how the content will be reviewed, as a matter of checking the transfer of ELMT skills to school governance. The methodology explains the tools used for data collection approaches, data organization, data analysis and interpretation.

Research Design

The research design was a qualitative methodology and case study was the approach with a concurrent triangulation strategy using qualitative data. The researcher examined in depth a program, an event, a process and individuals (Creswell, 2003). In this case school governance was the program with ELMT being the event and the transfer of ELMT skills to school governance was the process of investigation. The Headteachers and selected teachers in the schools were the individuals involved. This case study employed diverse types of strategies, ranging from interviewing and examining documents to evaluating the work environments (Merriam, 1998a). The approach allowed the opportunity "to understand a real – life phenomenon [transfer of ELMT skills to school governance] in depth" (Yin, 2009, p 18).

Headteachers hold the primary role of taking up new knowledge and skills they are exposed to in ELMT. The course aims of ELMT are assumed to empower the Headteachers with skills, to manage and lead the schools towards improving NEP. Each of the objectives has a theoretical underpinning, on how it can improve the quality of education when implemented in the school. However, it is the level of transfer of ELMT skills that will influence the school governance hence NEP trends. NEP being a key indicator, used by MoEST to determine school performance, can be used to relate the levels of transfer with the school performance. The exploration of the level of transfer brought forth how some of the topics in the business management aspects could have been implemented for effective governance.

ELMT is one of the PLS which is popular for the Headteachers. The content of the ELMT will determine which kind of skills the Headteachers will be exposed to. In this study, the focus will be ELMT offered by AKA, M. The ELMT is fully sponsored and is offered during school holidays and has in-situ sessions during the school term. This programme is offered in 360hrs over a period of 16 weeks. The review explored how the ELMT skills were being implemented in school governance, the levels of implementation (transfer of skills) were reviewed against the barriers faced and how the barriers were managed. The transfer of skills and the management of the barriers were analyzed against the business management skills, with the focus on presence of or the lack of these skills.

During the ELMT there are several ways to enhance the change to motivation. One key method is framing the development encountered either through the existence of a common understanding of leadership in the school (Mathieu & Martineau, 1997), reflective and experiential exercises during training (Moss et al, 1992) and/or the communication of rationale and support from TSC, MoEST or BOM (Birdi, Allan, & Warr, 1997). Such frameworks were implemented in the ELMT, so as to make the learning experiences personal and reflective to participants, who encouraged in them a positive and open attitude towards engaging to change, implementing is one aspect while exploring the impact of the training offered on understudy, of the impact of the approach.

Learner engagement is the extent to which participants are engaged in the process of building, applying and reflecting upon the capability to be mastered (Brown & Ford, 2002). ELMT is action-oriented, and provides a variety of experiential activities for Headteachers to try out and test out the skills learnt in their new knowledge and skills. The Headteachers are provided with timely constructive feedback. Feedback constitutes an important complement to these activities, because it informs participants about the effectiveness of their present learning strategies and prompts self-evaluations of progress toward attaining learning goals. The engagement during learning was explored through the deliverables produced by the respondents. The reflective journals, the action research report, the five year strategic plan, and monitoring reports were a clear indicator of determining the Headteachers' level of engagement.

The implementations of the ELMT skills were explored through the objectives of the ELMT. The objectives were examined through various tools which included interviews of teachers from classes 1, 3 and 6 as they represented lower, middle and higher primary levels. Focus group interviews were employed to the teachers, to explore how they perceived the Headteachers' leadership, networking of the school with stakeholders and team leadership of the Headteachers and barriers of transfer of ELMT skills. Although a focus group approach was implemented the nature of questions was designed to focus more on the activities the teachers participated in which were then reviewed to explore headteachers governance. There was questionnaire matrix that was filled by the Headteachers to check on their leadership styles, preferred leadership practices, horizontal leadership, transformational leadership and leading teams. The Headteachers' responses were compared with the teachers' responses to develop a deeper understanding on the level of transfer of ELMT skills on school governance.

The assumptions in the study were that the Headteachers gained their leadership skills through the professional learning sessions they attended which included ELMT. For a primary school Headteacher, the most accessible professional development is the certificate which is offered by AKU and AKAM and the diploma offered by KEMI. All the possible three courses have similarities in terms of the skill set, which they offer although they have some variances in scope, depth and duration. The effectiveness of the training is influenced by several factors, which include the design and the content. All the Headteachers involved in the study were exposed to ELMT, which was their sole education leadership training after attaining the headship.

According to Blumberg and Schindler (2008) consent to participate in a research, is not a straight forward matter and hence the Headteachers had to fill in consent forms in the research. The target population for this study was Headteachers from Mombasa County, Coast region who had attended ELMT four years back from the time of the study. A total of 40 Headteachers had attended the training in the last 4 years respectively. NEP Trends analysis was used to identify the schools for the research. NEP trends pre-and post ELMT (figure 1) were used to determine the schools to be selected and also guided the purposive stratified sampling for the study.

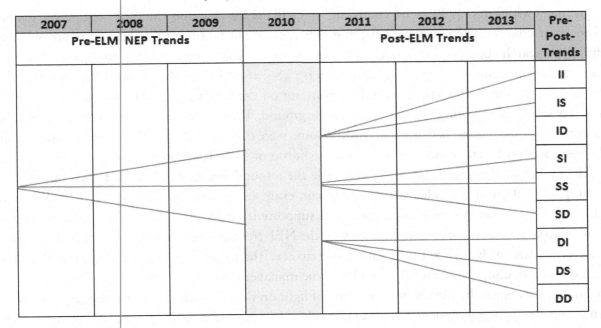

Figure 1. Graphical representation of the possibilities of NEP Pre and Post Trends scenarios (I-Increasing, S-Static, D-Decreasing)

Wango (2009) states that, "the assessment of schools in Kenya for quality, measures performance in terms of academic achievement through examination results, number of students who enroll [in secondary schools] and trends in school enrolment" p. 109. As identified by Wango, NEP trends were indicative of the level of impact, offered by the pre- and post-ELMT trends.

The exploration was done for two cohorts, one being 4 years after the training and another 3 years after the training. According to Johnson and Christensen (2008) this approach allowed the collection of diverse types of data to provide the best understanding for the research problem. In the current study the Headteachers were the trainees, the school was the organization and the TSC and MoEST were the managers who were assured to influence the transfer of ELMT skills (Newstrom, 1986). The variables were explored to determine how they influenced the transfer of ELMT skills.

The Headteachers were profiled, to collect data on their professional development over years of headship tenure. The school profiles were used to inform the school population, teacher population, student-teacher ratio and number of candidates. The identified Headteachers were observed and interviewed to understand how they governed the schools. The Headteachers were interviewed on their perception regarding what they perceived as challenges of the transfer of training and how they overcame the challenges.

Trend analysis will bring out trends in different categories such as increasing, static and decreasing NEP trends. Based on the outcomes of trends quota sampling was used to select schools from the increasing NEP trend groups (Meadows, 2003). Stratified random sampling was employed, to reflect the target population and reduce sampling variations (Meadows, 2003) as well as bias (Sun, 2009). This involved aspects like male and female Headteachers, urban and town schools among others.

Case study approach was deployed where ELMT was a case in a bound system. The focus was the Headteachers in the coastal county of Kenya with NEP being the case descriptor. The case study was explorative, due to multiple bounded systems involving multiple information and case based themes. Mariam (1998b) advocates for an explorative case study design in the field of education.

In agreement with Yin's (2009, p. 13) comment "you will use the case study method because you deliberately wanted to cover contextual conditions, believing that they might be highly pertinent to your phenomenon of study", the research approach deliberately selected contextual conditions (trainee Headteacher' professional portfolio and organization of school profile), managers (TSC and MoEST) based on the assumption that the other influencing factors on the trainer remained constant on the transfer of ELMT skills.

The study was meant to bring out the reality on the ground. The reality was that, from the NEP trends some schools were doing well; some had stagnated while some were dropping despite their Headteachers attending ELMT. These were the outcomes observed in the backdrop of ELMT, schools and respondents' professional profile. ELMT included content and objectives while the respondents' profile included years of experience in the headship. School profile included school enrolment, exam enrolment and staff deployment. The managers focused on TSC and MoEST who supervised and supported the Headteachers. The qualitative study was administered to strata identified so as to find out why the NEP trends were increasing post-ELMT and how they related to the transfer of ELMT skills in school governance. The focus was three variables, the Headteachers, schools and teachers since they were all under the same management.

The qualitative approach, allowed the shedding of light on the particular phenomenon (transfer of ELMT skills) in its natural setting (school governance) (Saunders, Lewis, & Thornhill, 2007). According to Henning, Van Rensburg and Smith (2004), the assumption underlying qualitative research is that knowledge is socially constructed. Hence, a qualitative approach was used to investigate transfer of ELMT skills, in school governance in a non-contrived situation with no manipulation of conditions.

Qualitative research does not seek to establish generalizations that are universal and context free (Gay and Airasian, 2000), but believes actions are strongly influenced by the context within which they occur. This research targeted a cohort of Headteachers who were governing schools after attending ELMT. Gay and Airasian acknowledge that the choice of the approach is also influenced by its inductive logic, where categories will emerge from Headteachers, teachers and schools rather than being pre-identified. This approach allowed production of rich content, bound information which leads to emergence of theories that helped explain the situation under study.

Research Questions

1. To what extent has the ELMT skills been transferred to school governance four years after attending ELMT?
2. What are the Headteachers perspectives of identified barriers of transfer?
3. What barriers are experienced by Headteachers as they transfer their skills to school governance?
4. How do Headteachers overcome the barriers they face during the transfer of the ELMT skills?

Population, Sampling Strategy, Sample Size

The total number of public primary schools in the coastal county is 115. The county is divided into four districts and 5 zones in each district. 40 Headteachers had attended ELMT from the county which was spread across districts and zones. The Headteachers were selected equally from the four districts and zones. To ensure population validity, a sample was randomly selected from all the Headteachers who attended ELMT in the last 4 years it included both genders, high and low population in the county. All focus group members met the inclusion criteria and their participation was voluntary. All the schools are in the urban region hence they were not discriminated on the regions. A total of four school Headteachers were selected based on the NEP trend analysis and gender balance. From each school a teacher was selected from lower, middle and upper bringing the total of the teachers interviewed to 12.

The sampling approach was based on purposive sampling to select cases which present increasing NEP trends between pre- and post-ELMT. This approach is referred to by Creswell (2007) as purposeful maximal sampling. The research was instrumental case study (Stake, 1995) because it focused on transfer of ELMT skills, to school governance in a selected bounded case which was Headteachers in the coastal county in Kenya. These methods concurred with Yin's (2009) description of a case being single, multi-cited focused on an issue.

First and foremost, the participants were willing to participate in the research and were selected when they acknowledged understanding what it entailed. The research strove to adopt an inductive stance and the structure, which was both quota samples as it accessed participants from the main group directly involved and purposive. These are participants who are considered best able to express informal opinions about school governance (Silverman 2001). Patton (1990) merits such sampling as it provides rich information for in-depth study of a case. The primary participants were the Headteachers and a balance on gender was employed to have equal numbers of male and female school Headteachers.

Secondary Participants

These were teachers in years 1, 3 and 6. These groups of teachers in one way or another experienced school governance; hence their involvement provided more data. These teachers have experienced the Headteachers' governance; hence they will be able to share their experiences, giving an insight of the extent to which the Headteachers had transferred their ELMT skills to school governance

Pilot Study

Prior to conducting the primary study, a pilot study was conducted to provide reliability for profiling, leadership (styles, preference, and networking), team (leadership and working together), barriers, organization impact and activities before, during and after training, open – ended interview protocol. Due to the size of the population, the pilot study was conducted to only 2 Headteachers, one from each of the cohorts and from both genders. The researcher visited the schools and interviewed the Headteachers, made notes on the artifacts and observed lessons in the schools. The interview recordings, the notes and the filled up forms were analyzed by the researcher. The pilot study allowed the researcher to become familiar with administrating instruments: the forms and the open ended interviews made the essential changes to streamline and improve the administration of the primary study. There were no changes made to the forms as this had been validated by the designers. However, the open-ended questionnaires were adjusted for clarity and contextual realities.

The emergent, generalized statements from the findings were evaluated again through checks on the data. Observations, statements or similar pieces of data were interpreted in different ways, to provide the most plausible explanation for any analyzed data (Marshall & Rossman, 1999). The questions were developed, tested and gradually improved during piloting. The piloting was done in a context similar to the study context, in terms of structure and composition but in a different geographical location. The piloting involved taking participants, interviewing them and comparing the responses with the objectives of the interviews. Amendments were made in the questions to achieve the objectives with clarity.

Participants Consent

The consent forms were designed in accordance to Creswell (2003) minimum request of the following elements.

a) A brief explanation for the purpose of the interview and study.
b) Length of time to conduct the interview.
c) Language stating participation is voluntary and they could leave the research at any time without any consequences.
d) Right to ask questions
e) Process to review the transcripts.
f) Explain how data, identity privacy and confidentiality will be maintained.
g) Permission to record the interview.
5. Signature lines for both interviewee and researcher agreeing to the terms of the consent were not required.

A letter of information and the consent form were sent to the participants. The participants and the researcher signed the informed consent form prior to completing any instruments. Copies of and researcher's bill of rights were also provided to the participants and the informed consent form.

Data Collection Methods

Data collection involved drawing from multiple sources of information such as interviews, artifacts, documents (current/archival records) and observations (direct/participants). Analysis involved data organization, to identify emerging themes, so as to understand the complexity of the case. This case study data handling methods, led to meaning making of the case. The interpretive phase, reported on the learning about the transfer of ELMT skills on school governance. The identified Headteachers from the NEP analysis were shadowed, observed and interviewed, to understand how they implemented the ELMT skills.

In order to investigate barriers overcoming factors, qualitative methods seemed most appropriate to gather Headteachers viewpoints, their experiences and to some extent the relationships between these viewpoints and their practice. Data from the study was generated through naturalistic approaches such as semi structured interviews, field notes; i.e. observations within and around the school, collection of documents and artifacts (McGee-Brown 1994; Merriam, 1998a; Stake, 1994).

Interviews

For the questionnaire and open- ended interviews, the meeting took place at an agreed location, which was conducive to open and candid communication. To conduct the interview, the researcher arrived at the interview site prepared with resources. Throughout the interview the researcher recorded and took supporting notes. Following the interview, the researcher transcribed the recordings, reviewed the notes and linked them to the interview questions. The recordings were transcribed immediately after the interview. An interview transcript was provided to the participants for review, revisions and approval, along with the researcher's comments. If there were clarifications or revisions on the interview transcript they were made by the participants in writing immediately they received the transcript documents.

The Headteachers were interviewed and data was recorded and transcribed. Although the Headteachers were principal respondents, the review of the interviews would identify any other involved potential respondents. Forms were used to explore leadership, teamwork, learning environments, organizational culture and networking.

Interviews were conducted on one-on-one basis and lasted 30-45 minutes. The limitations of the timing were bound by the fact that the teachers accepted interviews only during school time and the lessons were 55 min in length. The interviews were scheduled as shown in Table 8

Table 8 *Participants Interview Frequency*

Number	Participant	Frequency
4	Headteacher	5
12	Teacher	2
12	Teachers in a focus Group	3

As for Hammersley-Fletcher (2004) this system of repeat interviewing allowed for re-focusing at the end of each week and the development of new questions through issues raised, by the participants themselves.

Semi structured, open-ended interviews were used; Wellington (2000) asserts that in semi structured interviews, the interviewer is flexible to ask questions in any order. The questions adopted a positive stance, with the main prompt to explore how they perceived their Headteachers' transfer their ELMT skills on school governance. Times permitting further prompts were asked on the leadership and how they could improve their school programs. The prompting was directed to derive the barriers the Headteachers were experiencing and how they were managing the barriers. The Headteachers were interviewed 5 times with the final interview conducted at the conclusion of the study. The culminating interview allowed the researcher to review key issues and clarify issues raised by the teachers such as strict governance by the Headteachers.

Focused Group Interview

Teachers were interviewed in a focus group. Given the heavy demands on teachers; three teachers from lower middle and upper primary were interviewed in focus groups. Patton (1990) advocates for this approach, as it has an objectivity of getting high quality data in a social context where people can consider their own views in the context of views of the others. The focus group technique was utilized, because it is the most important and popular qualitative research tool in any exploratory study (Denzin & Lincoln, 1994). Moreover Robson (2002) adds that contributions can be encouraged from people who are reluctant or feel they have nothing to say. Lasting 45–70 minutes, the sessions were facilitated by the Master trainers who have qualification in educational research they did not belong to the school and had not interviewed the Headteachers. The sessions were done in the school in a quiet room and they were recorded and later transcribed to be confirmed by the teachers before processing. This 'outsider' audience was intended to encourage the teachers to articulate ideas which might otherwise have been taken for granted in the areas of school governance, networking and team work. The focus group interview went well and it was very instrumental as the participants reinforced each other's responses (Patton, 1990). However, during the interview there were initial challenges faced, when some of the participants tried to dominate the proceedings. This was managed through directing questions to individuals in turn and letting others fill in. One thing learnt with focus group was that it was important to give the guidelines upfront of how the sessions were conducted. Another finding was the importance of involving all the participants in the discussions. Robson (2002) cautions on the size to be within three and five and also the facilitation need to be well managed. This was adhered to with the groups focusing on lower, middle and upper primary teachers in each case.

After each interview session, a summary was prepared. The summary contained the focus questions, emerging themes, any interesting or illumination thing and implications for subsequent data collection. This summary served as data reduction strategy. Before subsequent interviews the issues raised in the summary were addressed and a copy of the transcript was shared with the participants for validation.

Observation

In addition to interviews, there were observations in several areas like classrooms, staffroom, departmental meetings, and interaction among respondents. Observation checklists were designed and used for observations. Field notes were developed from what was seen, heard or experienced in the course of the research. Robson (2002) advocates for observation as a direct technique, as data from observation can often complement information obtained through other means. Headteachers were observed for a day, allowing for some collaboration of how they were governing the school. The Headteachers were shadowed for a day and the teachers were observed three times. The combination of these methods enabled a triangulation of the Headteachers' responses. The Headteachers were shadowed for a day and observed how they influenced the running of the school. The observations were typed and saved together with the summary. This facilitated quick reference, through word search and the summary captured issues gathered or missed in the observation. From the summary further areas for observations were identified. The combination of these methods enabled a triangulation between the Headteachers' responses on school governance perceptions, ideas and the reality of their roles. Robson elaborates further by saying; observation might be used to validate o messages obtained by interviews. Hence the observations were used to provide verification of the interview data.

Artifact analysis

This involved the documents which were related to school governance directly or indirectly. It also involved analysis of the resources that were facilitating school governance. Marshall and Rossman (1999) recommend observations, to include "systematic motion and recording of artifacts in the social setting" (p.78). Artifacts were analyzed and where possible school permission was requested to make copies or photographs of the artifacts. Artifacts were analyzed in the course of the research to verify the interview data and also to provide more information. Glesne (1999) advised that artifacts are enriched by what was seen and heard by supporting, expanding and challenging the researchers' portrayals and perceptions. The analysis of the artifacts involved what Merriam (1998a) referred to as systematic procedure for the content in the artifacts. She further credits the approach, because documentary material is stable, unlike interviewing or observation, the presence of the investigator does not alter what is to be studied. However, she cautions the interpretation of the researcher, has a crucial role to play in reconstructing meaning. Artifacts such as school mission, supervision reports, TOR's, School timetable were analyzed. In each artifact a content analysis criterion was developed. For example, the school time table was to identify the Head teacher's engagement in teaching and learning, the visitor's book was to track the stakeholders who were visiting the school. Other documents analyzed were the School inspection reports, the BOM minutes of meeting, Headteachers' classroom observation sheets, staff meeting minutes, the school strategic plan and school reports on national examinations. Artifacts such as staff meetings minutes, school inspection report, PTA and BOM meeting minutes, staff hand book, classroom observation, notes by Headteachers and strategic planning schedule, visitors books and the time table. The minutes will bring out what is discussed in the meeting. The classroom observation notes would indicate what the Headteachers sees and how he supports the teachers. The school inspection reports will bring out the frequency and nature of feedback the school receives from the inspector. The strategic plan schedule would indicate the people involved and how they plan for the school. The time table would indicate how the school is run. The staff hand book would bring out the responsibilities of the teachers hence show empowerment and delegation. The visitor's books would indicate the networking partners and their role in the school. A document was prepared to clarify the context and significance as well as summarizing the contents of lengthy documents.

Data Collection Instruments

The instruments included but were not limited to leadership forms, interview protocol, observation protocol and artifacts analysis protocol. Triangulation strengthens the research study by utilizing multiple methods and approaches (Breakwell, Hammond, Fife-Schaw, & Smith, 2006). The researcher integrated qualitative instruments, to provide voice and understanding of the phenomenon being examined (Creswell, 2008). Detailed descriptive field notes were kept for planned and incidental observations. Interpretations were made from the analysis to arrive at a response to the research question.

The professional data and school profile data were used to get information about the school in terms of the resources in the school as well as performance. The performance was used to understand the NEP trends before and after ELMT training. This was used to select the schools which were to be studied under qualitative approach.

School governance tool was used to explore the understanding of the Headteachers on the ten aspects, which they were supposed to have gained through the ELMT. Then it was also used to explore what they were implementing in their day to day life. The analysis involved comparing the understanding with the actual content to help get to know their level of understanding and the application was to find out how much of what they had learnt could be applied, so this was used to find the level of application of what they had learnt. The Headteachers' leadership in general was used to explore the leadership and this was important as it was used to triangulate what the Headteachers had said, as they were applying in day to day life and what the teachers saw in the leadership of the Headteachers. This was a tool used on the teachers in a focus group, to understand the leadership of the Headteachers in the school. Transformational leadership was one of the key elements in ELMT, which was used to understand the kind of leadership that the Headteachers were going through. This was checking whether there are transformational leaders because at the end of the training, the Headteachers were expected to be. The other aspect of leadership is horizontal leadership, this was used to check the level of the leadership in school, whether it is top level down or it is distributed.

The Headteachers were exposed to different leadership styles where by a questionnaire was used to explore the predominant style, in which the Headteachers were undergoing. This tool was used to analyze which type of leadership the Headteachers were displaying and this was done hand in hand with the preference in leadership styles, this was done to understand the trend in terms of the leadership of the Headteachers because at the end of the day the Headteachers were supposed to transverse from being managers to leaders, so the tool under preference to leadership was used to understand the level of transition to leadership.

Leadership matrix was to understand the leadership of the Headteachers in the leadership matrix, where the leadership was situated and the analysis involved mapping that particular leadership and putting it into quadrants in the leadership. Team work was used to explore the kind of teams which are established in the school and this was used by teachers as well as the Headteachers themselves to understand the kind of teams in schools as team work is one of the aspect taught in ELMT. Team leadership was used to check and find out the level of leadership the Headteachers were doing in terms of teams and to harness team spirit through working with others, was used to explain how interactions in the schools was happening in terms of the team learning environment. There were classroom and lesson observations to see if teaching and learning were influenced by the school governance. In ELMT, networking was one of the elements whereby the Headteachers were led to be able to network. Therefore networking was used for teachers and Headteachers to understand how they engaged with the network, in terms of stake holders working in the school. Transfer of training was used to identify what was ranking high in terms of barriers, to transfer by training as well as what they consider important during, after and before training. Organizational barriers for training was used in order to identify what barriers there were in organizational structure, which was making the transfer of training a problem and this was to understand how the organization was affecting the transfer of training.

Trainee action was used to look at what the Headteachers were doing before, after and during the training, to understand and take up in the training. Then the Headteachers were interviewed generally to explore their perspectives on the implementation and perspectives on the barriers, while they were doing their training. These are the tools that were used to collect data, to understand the skills for ELMT and put them to practice. A data collection schedule was used to implement the tools.

Reflective Journal

Throughout the research, the researcher maintained a reflective journal. It informed the researcher on the methodology and provided guidance in understanding any critical incidences that would occur during the course of the studies (Shepherd, 2004). Memos within the journal provided more information on the interpretations made along the research.

Researcher Role, Bias and Experience

Unaeza and Gioko (2010) observe that familiarization with the context and the content of research enables the researcher to be able to have insightful experience in data collection and meaning making process. The researcher's experience in schools and in teacher training provided competence. Hence, the role of the researcher was to capture the situation as it was and present the meaning making process to allow natural generalization by the readers.

Researchers are ethically obliged to possess a high level of competence and skill in undertaking a research. The researcher has been a lecturer for 4 years in a tertiary institution (1993-1997), a secondary school teacher for sixteen years (1997-2014), 3 years (2009-2014) as a coordinator in a professional development center and has completed substantial 2 years (2012- 2014) as a vice principal in charge of professional development and outreach. The researcher has a research experience in research methodology both at graduate and post graduate level. At the coordination level the researcher has facilitated the training of 1688 primary school teachers through literacy, numeracy, pedagogy, technology integration, educational leadership and management training. The researcher has trained 112 Headteachers from two counties on educational leadership and management from 2009 to 2013. The researcher targets to train over 125 Headteachers in the counties by 2017. The researchers' cohort was not part of the research to avoid bias. The researcher is competent and experienced in handling a research of this magnitude.

Credibility

There were attempts to strengthen the validity of the findings by further eliciting participant validation. The researcher strived to achieve rigor in the research by triangulation through methodology (Cohen & Manion, 2000), pilot testing, constantly analyzing the data in the process, seeking participants' views on interpretations, and using a variety of methods to understand the phenomenon. Although experiences had shown that school governance was socially constructed, the researcher avoided a deductive approach. In some instances when transcription was taken to the participants for credibility, they altered some information they had said earlier. This changed the interpretation of data; ethically the researcher took the changes made and as a researcher there was a feeling that some valuable data was lost. However, according to Tappan (2001) validity and truth of claims from this perspective was established through agreement, rather than empirical tests: "if the… [participant] agreed on what a text means, based on… biases, assumptions, prejudices, and values, then that interpretation is considered to be "true" or "valid" (p. 52). The knowledge was not bound by the researchers' interpretation and understanding of the transfer of ELMT skills to school governance, but together with the participants, they created a descriptive body of knowledge about the Headteachers' experiences in ELMT skills transfer to school governance, which is neither subjective nor objective but intersubjective and thus conceptually true for both parties (Kvale, 1996). These approaches were more concerned with relatability, which Stake (1994) views as "the purpose is not to represent the world, but the case" (p. 245).

Organization of Data

Pseudonyms were adapted from official designations, and the corresponding abbreviated codes were used henceforth to indicate sources for quoted material. The data was organized with the major framework of levels of implementation, barriers and approaches of overcoming the barriers. A data recording chart was developed, for the three categories of data collection interview transcripts, observations, and artifact analysis. Miles and Huberman (1994) suggest several schemas of recording qualitative data. The techniques streamlined data management; however it was not to be fixed so as to accommodate serendipitous findings.

Data organization started with a folder on the computer for the data management. It contained the template for the contact and summary sheet for the observation, interviews and artifacts. This was done to view the whole structure, so that data could be tracked as it was appended. After each session of data collection the template was filled up and printed out. The interviews were listened to and transcribed. The transcribed data was read through as the recording was replayed to check for accuracy. The transcription was then returned to the respondent to read and confirm that what was transcribed is what they said and whether they wanted to add, clarify or change any statement. The summary sheet was then filled and printed. Soft copies and the sound file were sent to a remote location and another saved in a portable device. After a week of data collection the folder was burned on a CD and kept separately in a locked cabinet. This proved crucial for safety and access of data from remote locations. The sound files for interviews were saved in the same folders alongside the transcribed format. Each transcription had the voice format attached for verification (Fig. 2) and each file had a descriptive name {[No] __ [data source] _ [Participant] _ [Session]} (Fig. 3). The files were then imported into a spread sheet for the purpose of coding and criterion based filtration.

Miles and Herberman (1994) suggest several schemas of recording qualitative data. The techniques streamlined data management; however it was not fixed so as to accommodate serendipitous findings. Pole and Lampard (2002) observe that during data collection, processual data analysis occurs because the researcher is continuously engaged with the data as it is collected. Pole and Lampard further explain that processual analysis is important in informing data collection and in shaping the direction of a research project. This means that data analysis will continue with data collection progressing.

Interview 2 Headteacher 005.3ga

INTERVIEW 005. HEADTEACHER.

1. By 1978 PTA was silenced in primary school and only active in sec(powerful is the SMC.

2. Role of SMC.
   - Recommend discipline in children

Figure 2 Transcriptions with embedded file and data file list

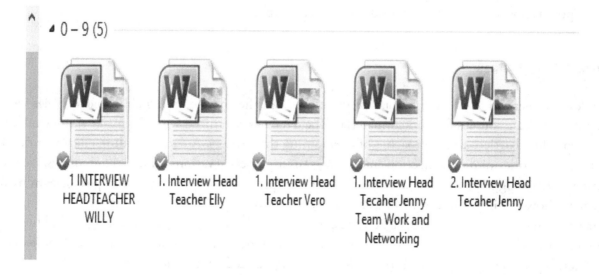

Figure 3 Descriptive files names

Analyzing Data

Data analysis was time consuming and a complex process which included making sense of questionnaire responses, interview transcripts, observations, and artifacts analyzed. All the data (interviews, questionnaires, observation notes and artifact analysis) were reviewed first in a general manner, to obtain a sense of the data and emerging themes. The data received from interviews was prepared, organized and transcribed. Upon completion of the transcription process, the data was analyzed into themes through a process of open-coding (Strauss & Corbin, 2007). Open coding is defined as the process of "naming and categorizing of a phenomenon through close examination of data" (Strauss & Corbin, 2007, p. 62). Phrases/themes were categorized as the unit of analysis. Software was used to search for key words and filter the paragraphs (Gioko, 2007). This procedure enabled a thorough and systematic search for chunks of information. Analysis was conducted to identify patterns, trends, and responses to the research question. This provided structure to the gathered data and allowed for triangulation between the various research instruments used. The data represented in figures, tables, and/or discussions for interpretation. Data was then coded for analysis according to the method of qualitative data analysis. To ensure validity and utility/usefulness of the data, they were checked by a second researcher (peer reviewer) who verified the coding system used and the results.

The analysis of the data embraced both the emic and etic approach. As Lett (1990) explains, from an anthropological perspective, "Emic constructs are accounts, descriptions, and analyses expressed in terms of the conceptual schemes and categories regarded as meaningful and appropriate by the native members of the culture whose beliefs and behaviors are being studied" (p. 130). This allowed putting aside the theories and assumptions in order to let the participants and data to speak and allow themes, patterns and concept emerge. The grounded approach enabled the particularity of the context under research, respecting the local viewpoints and its potential to uncover the unexpected findings. This was applied on what the Headteachers thought they were implementing. The etic approach used theories of transfer of training and the barriers faced from literature review. According to Lett (1990) "Etic constructs are accounts, descriptions, and analyses expressed in terms of the conceptual schemas and categories regarded as meaningful and appropriate by the community of scientific observers" (p. 130). The existing theory or conceptual framework of transfer of training and barriers was used to see if it applied to the Kenyan Headteachers at the coastal county, who had undertaken ELMT. The approach allowed for comparison across contexts and populations, and the development of more general cross-cultural concepts (Morris, Leung, Ames, & Lickel, 1999).

Generating Categories, Theme and Patterns

The next step was to read and re-read the data between five to ten times in order to develop a clear picture of governance in the school (Lincon and Guba, 2000). Constant comparative method (Strauss, 1987) was used to identify salient themes, recurring ideas or language and patterns that linked the respondents to the setting which Lincon and Guba refer to as naturalistic inquiry "challenges" or "support" was used. Through questioning the data like "some teachers embrace the new approaches" and reflecting on the conceptual framework, similarities and differences were sought. The emerging themes and patterns were identified and used as a guideline to code the data. Thematic units were identified, compared and discussed (Merriam. 1998b; Yin, 2009).

The use of criteria based data, filter word and sentence search in the database reduced the time in handling the data. For example, if a criterion was teachers' responses a criterion was established like "identifying the teams" and the expression was used to search in the database. Subsequent, searches were done until emerging themes and patterns were identified from the data.

Grouping these ideas into themes or broad categories allowed the researcher to interpret the data adequately. This technique of analyzing qualitative data is known as the scissor-and-sort method and is the most common technique used by qualitative researchers (Denzin& Lincoln, 1994). The themes were used to develop codes such as "ITP" for internal teacher practice with the subcategory "PIB" for perspective in barriers. The data was filtered looking for statement that fit the codes. Each data item found was tagged with the code. Thematic units were identified, compared and discussed (Merriam, 1998b; Yin 2003). Sometimes data elements were found to fall in several categories, at this point a resolution was found based on literature.

Coding the Data

The preliminary sets of theme were used to code additional data. Emerging themes were added to the preliminary coding scheme, if something kept recurring and it was not in the code-set, a new code was established and added to protect against projection and ensure reliability of coding scheme, an explicit code of theme labels, definitions and examples was developed (Boyatzis, 1998). Subsequent coding was done using the explicit theme labels and definitions.

Date	Name	Perspective in Barriers	Theme 1	Theme 2
HEAD TEACHER INTERVIEW 4-Perspective on Barriers				
2/27/2014	Elly	Case in court between the Baptist church and the government as to who owns the school.	Policy	Conflict
2/13/2014	Jenny	And the other one I can say it's just routine and tradition which was there. There was no that follow up activity and the idea of being now told "can you reflect the whole week, how the lessons are" it's an addition of more work. They feel as if we are disturbing them. "Mwalimuanatusumbua" you know?	Culture	Commitment
2/6/2014	Vero	There was no reading culture it's now coming up.	Culture	Reading
2/6/2014	Vero	Outside destructions for example cows and goats brought to feed in school	Culture	External

Figure 4. Drop down list for codes in the data base

Figure 4 shows the codes as they were used in filtering data. The code set was the drop down menu with codes like, internal as the base code, participants and focus as the secondary codes. Through the data base chunks of paragraphs were allocated the codes, some fell in two or three categories. With the data base it was easy to maintain the codes, since the codes used were maintained in a database.

Testing Emergent Understanding

The emergent, generalized statements from the findings were evaluated again through thorough checks on the data. Observations, statements or similar pieces of data may be interpreted in different ways to provide the most plausible explanation for any analyzed data (Marshall & Rossman, 1999).

Searching for Alternatives

For the categories and patterns that seemed so apparent, other plausible explanations and linkages were found, for such situations where majority were in agreement over an issue, but some thought differently. The alternatives to each explanation, the interpretations were based on the concepts such as organizational theories, structure, policies and procedures, purposes, goals, and requirements of position (Clegg & Hardy, 1996; Elmore, 1995; Senge, 1990; Van Sell, Brief, & Schuler, 1981). Relationships among external and internal environmental factors as presented in systems theory (Scott, 1992); Micro political concepts such as power, influence and resource allocation (Mawhinney, 1999).

Summary

The research design was a case study which entailed a qualitative approach with a concurrent triangulation strategy using qualitative data. Headteachers hold the primary role of taking up new knowledge and skills they are exposed to in ELMT. The implementations of the ELMT skills were explored through the objectives of the ELMT. The assumptions in the study were that the Headteachers gained their leadership skills through PLS they attended where ELMT was one of them. The exploration was done for two cohorts, one being 4 years after the training and another 3 years after the training. The Headteachers were profiled to collect data on their professional development over the years and their years of tenure as Headteachers were used to. Trend analysis will bring out trends in different categories, such as increasing, static and decreasing NEP trends. Case study approach was deployed, where ELMT was a case in a bounded system that is, Headteachers in the coastal county of Kenya with NEP being the case descriptor. The outcome of the qualitative study was bound to reflect the reality on the ground. The qualitative approach allowed the shedding of light on the particular phenomenon (transfer of ELMT skills) in its natural setting (school governance). Qualitative research does not seek to establish generalizations that are universal and context free.

The total number of public primary schools in the coastal county was 115. The county was divided into four districts and 5 zones in each district. The sampling approach was based on purposive sampling to select cases which present increasing NEP trends, between pre- and post-ELMT. First and foremost, the participants were willing to participate in the research and were selected when they acknowledged that they understood what the participation entailed. The teachers involved were in years 1, 3 and 6. These groups of teachers in one way or another experienced the school governance hence, their involvement enriched the data. Prior to conducting the primary study, a pilot study was conducted to provide reliability for profiling, leadership (styles, preference, and networking), team (leadership and working together), barriers, organization impact and actions before, during and after training and open – ended interview protocol. The emergent, generalized statements from the findings were evaluated again through checks on the data.

Data collection involved drawing from multiple sources of information such as interviews, artifacts, documents (current/archival records) and observations (direct/participants). For the questionnaire and open-ended interviews, the meetings took place at an agreed location, which was conducive to open and candid communication. The Headteachers were interviewed and data was recorded and transcribed. Interviews were conducted on one-on-one basis and lasted 30 - 45 mins. Semi structured and open-ended interviews were used. Teachers were interviewed in a focus group given the heavy demands on teachers; the three teachers from lower middle and upper primary were interviewed in focus groups. After each interview session a summary was prepared. In addition to interviews, there were observations in several areas like classrooms, staffroom, departmental meetings, and interaction among respondents. This involved the documents which were related to school governance directly or indirectly. The instruments included but were not limited to leadership forms, interview protocol, observation protocol and artifacts analysis protocol. Throughout the research, the researcher maintained a reflective journal.

Unaeza and Gioko (2010) observe that familiarization with the context and the content of research enables the researcher to be able to have insightful experience in data collection and meaning making process. There were attempts to strengthen the credibility of the findings by further eliciting participant validation.

Pseudonyms were adapted from official designations, and the corresponding abbreviated codes were used henceforth to indicate sources for quoted material. The data was organized with the major framework of levels of implementation, barriers and approaches of overcoming the barriers. Data analysis was time consuming and a complex process which included making sense of forms filled, questionnaire responses, interview transcripts, observations, and artifacts analyzed. The emergent generalized statements from the findings were evaluated again through thorough checks on the data. For the categories and patterns that seem so apparent, other plausible explanation and linkages were found for such situations where majority were in agreement over an issue, but some thought differently.

Chapter 4: Analysis and presentation of results

This chapter presents the findings of the study. The chapter shares the demographics and profile of the participating schools and Headteachers. In this chapter there are presentations of the findings on school leadership, teams, networking and the extent of implementing ELMT skills by the Headteachers. The chapter thereafter looks at the ranking of Newstrom's barriers by the Headteachers, the barriers identified by the Headteachers and their actions before, during and after the ELMT training. Finally the chapter presents how the Headteachers have tried to overcome the barriers on ELMT skills transfer as well as how the business management skills could be implemented to help.

Demographic Statistics

15 forms were returned out of the 40 sent to the Headteachers. This represented 35% of the cohort. The analysis of the NEP results over the eight years was generally reducing which reflected the national trends. The NEP trends over the eight years for the 15 school ranged between -0.002 and -33.93. Over the eight years the rate of change of the mean score was -5.29 with the mean averaging at 234.15 out of a possible maximum of 500. The analysis of pre- and post ELMT NEP trends brought out four Headteachers whose NEP trends were improving when compared pre- post-NEP.

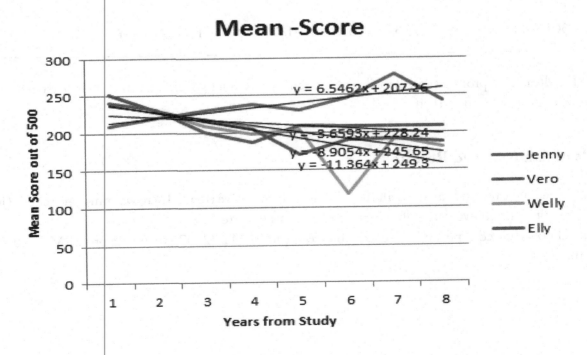

Figure 5 Mean Score Trends for the four schools

School Profiles

Four schools were identified to be having improving post ELMT NEP trends. The four Headteachers identified were 2 females and 2 males. 1 female was from the first cohort hence she had been implementing the skills for four years while the 2 males and 1 female were from the second cohort which had been implementing the skills in the last three years. Table 9 shows the demographic of the schools' data. Within the schools, 12 teachers were identified with four each from class 1, 3 and 6.

Table 9 *The demographic of the schools involved in the study*

Head-teacher Name	Aspect so of the school														
	No. of boys	No of Girls	No. of female teachers	No. of male teachers	No. of exam Candidates boys	No. of exam candidates girls	Avg. Mean Scores. 05'-12	No. of classrooms	No. of toilets	Library	Open field for physical education	Perimeter wall	Science lab	Computer Lab.
Welly	396	406	13	8	80	66	198.18	10	4	N	Y	Y	N	N
Eli	516	525	19	4	71	83	205.57	12	21	Y	Y	N	N	N
Jenny	303	216	15	4	41	22	248.96	16	21	Y	Y	Y	N	N
Vero	364	402	11	2	34	51	211.78	8	4	N	Y	N	N	N

The Headteachers' profiles presented their experiences in school governance and their perspectives of the main challenges they faced in their schools.

Details of Analysis and Results

Over the eight year trends analysis all the schools had a negative trend. There was only one school (Jenny's) that had a positive trend over the eight years trend analysis (Figure 5).

Four schools showed a positive difference between pre-ELMT (2007-2010) and pre-ELMT (2010-2013) (Figure 6).

NEP-Trends

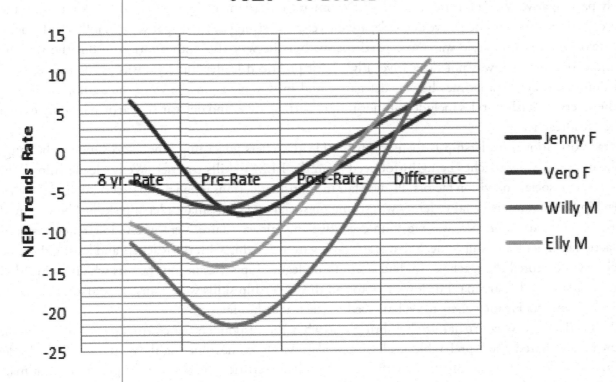

Figure 6. NEP Trends (8 Years, Post-, Pre-ELMT and Difference)

The NEP trends over the eight years for the 15 schools ranged between -0.002 and -33.93. Over the eight years the rate of change of the mean score was -5.29 with the mean averaging at 234.15 out of a possible maximum of 500. Only one school had a positive trend over the eight years. A comparison of pre and pre-ELMT brought out four schools that had an improving NEP trends.

Extent of Implemented ELMT Skills in School Governance

The exploration of the level of implementation of the ELMT skills in the schools brought out key aspects of leadership, teams and networking. The three aspects addressed leadership, working as teams and reaching out to stakeholders. Furthermore the Headteachers provided what they had implemented through open ended questionnaire and guided content based questioning basing their perspectives on what they understand and what they had implemented.

Headteachers Governance

School governance influenced by the school leadership. The leadership of the Headteachers was evaluated exploring the style of leadership, leadership skills, horizontal nature of the leadership, transformational leadership, working with others and Headteachers' perspectives about their leadership.

Leadership styles varied across a spectrum from authoritarian to laser-faire. The styles of leadership impacted how the Headteachers influenced the teachers with new approaches to governance. Vero's leadership style was mostly participative with a fair time as delegative and authoritarian. Welly was found to operate on leadership styles of authoritarian, participative and delegative. Welly was strong in participative style followed by delegative style. Jenny's leadership style was more participative but she was also authoritarian. From the interviews it was indicative that she was not delegative. Ely's most practiced leadership style was participative. He had a clear dominant style, sometimes he was delegative and in rare occasions he wore the authoritarian hat. The Headteachers leadership styles included authoritarian, participative, and delegative. Participative style cut across all the Headteachers.

Transformational leadership is focused on the Headteachers governing schools to support the long term uptake of the new approaches being introduced from the ELMT skills transfer. Welly's leadership skills were very strong on social and vision factors. He was fair in charismatic, transactional and execcussions. Welly's lowest leadership factor was laissez faire. Jenny was strong on social and charisma leadership skills. She was moderate on vision and transaction. She was weak on executive and laissez – faire. Vero was visionary, charismatic and transactional in her leadership style. She was struggling in socializing with the teachers and letting them be free. She closely monitored the teachers. Eli had strength on leadership styles in four factors which included vision, social excursion and charisma. His lowest factor on the leadership skills were transactional and laissez – faire. The ELMT targets Headteachers to be balanced in the leadership factors.

Perspectives are very crucial as they bring out what the respondents preferred according to them. The Headteachers shared their preferable leadership styles. Welly comes out highly in terms of the leadership attributes. Welly was very comfortable with leadership characteristics and skills. Vero preferred what made her an educator and a leader. Jenny's perception on leadership and practice indicated that she understood what leadership is and what she was supposed to do. Ely's preferred leadership style indicated that he is on the way to becoming a leader.

The Headteachers' styles of leadership were also viewed through a matrix of people vs. tasks. The leadership matrix was used to map the task and people foci by the Headteachers' leadership. Vero's leadership fell in to team leadership where she is both strong on people task and people skills (7, 8.4). Welly's leadership fell in the team leadership quadrant (8.2, 7.2). Ely's leadership fell just slightly into team leadership at (5.6, 6.8). Jenny's leadership is at low end of team leadership (6.0, 6.4). She was beginning to get strong in both people and task. She was moderately a strong leader and had ideas on what was required in terms of practice. The matrix in Figure 7 presented the Headteachers status post-ELMT showing a gradual improvement after exposure to ELMT.

Headteachers are leaders who have followers to govern. The Headteachers had to measure their strengths in behaviors that are essential to human relations. Vero was very strong in the attributes of interest such as self – exploration, feelings, genuineness, immediacy, empathy, self – disclosure. However she did not respect people whose work she did not approve. Jenny was strong on feelings, genuineness and immediacy. Jenny was however weak in confrontation and self-disclosure. Ely was strong on genuineness and confrontation. He was however weak in feeling and initiatives. Welly was strong in self-exploration, empathy, concreteness and immediacy. He was however weak on respect. Behaviors essential for human relations were exhibited uniquely by each of the Headteachers. As leaders, Headteachers were supposed to influence the teachers and lead and guide them. Their strength in behaviors essential in human relations reflected how they influenced the teachers in the schools (Fig 6).

The Headteachers' leadership styles included authoritarian, participative, and delegative. Participative style cut across all the Headteachers. The Laissez faire style did not appear for any of the Headteachers.

Transformational leadership identified the Headteachers as strong in social and vision factors. The preferred leadership brought out all the Headteachers as being in leadership or tending towards leadership. The leadership matrix placed all the Headteachers in the Team Leadership category. Although they were in this category some were just entering the categories while the others were more developed in the category. The Headteachers displayed different strengths in human relationships. Strengths were in genuineness, self-exploration, empathy, correctness and immediacy. Mid-levels human relationships were confrontation and initiative. Self-disclosure, feelings and respect were weak areas expressed by the Headteachers.

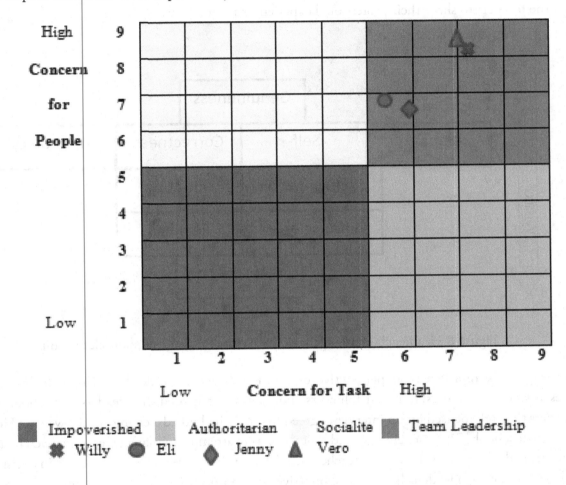

Figure 7. Leadership Matrix

Teachers' perspective of Headteachers' leadership

The teachers explored the Headteachers leadership in several aspects which included teaching, professional learning, meeting, gender issues and school development plans. The teachers felt that they were supported by the Headteachers. They noted that the Headteachers visited their classes although some shared that they did not see the importance of class visits by the Headteachers. There was also cover for lessons when some teachers were absent. Team teaching happened in schools and the Headteachers were there to discuss issues related to teaching. The Headteachers supported professional learning and teachers were sent to such sessions and given opportunities to share after the sessions. The Headteachers had meetings and they were participatory by all teachers which included exploring on how to make teaching and learning better. The Headteachers ensured gender was catered for which included inclusion, mixed groups and gender responsive rules and activities. The teachers felt their strength as they were involved in the school development plans and strategic plans and shared their thoughts and ideas for the plan. This allowed the teachers to be part of problem solving. The teachers' perspective of the school, governance was important so as to compare with Headteachers' responses on how the school was governed. It was evident from the teachers that the Headteachers were practicing pedagogical leadership. The teachers spoke about the Headteachers observing their lessons. Furthermore, the Headteachers allowed the teachers to share their professional experiences in meetings.

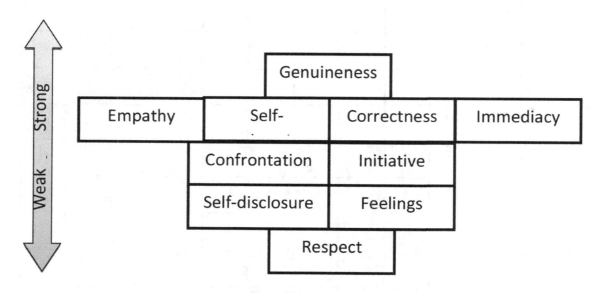

Figure 8 Headteachers strengths on behaviors for good human relationship

The teachers were asked their perspective on the Headteacher's leadership. This was for triangulation purposes as well as to understand their followers and how they regarded their leaders and school governance. The teachers through focused group interview agreed that they had noted a change in the way the Headteachers governed their schools. The teachers observed that there were attempts to manage resources well hence students and teachers had access to resources. The teachers also felt that they were now more involved in decision making. The teachers found the Headteachers more supportive and approachable; however the teachers expressed some biasness on the Headteachers' preferable treatment to some teachers. The teachers felt that they needed more classroom observation and constructive feedback from the Headteachers. Although the teachers noticed change and felt empowered they observed that more could be done to make them better teachers.

According to the teachers, the Headteachers had changed on their leadership. There was an element of support, inclusion and empowerment of the teachers by the Headteachers. The Headteachers were working closely with the teachers involving them in both solving problems and school developmental plan. There were changes observed in the Headteachers' governance some of which included resource management. The teachers claimed that the Headteachers were biased when in their classroom observation and wished they could have more support in classroom observation and feedback.

Classroom practice as reflection on governance

The Headteachers are trained through ELMT to be pedagogical leaders; hence their governance should be reflected on the quality of teaching in the school. Classrooms were observed on the basis of what the teachers could control. The aspects of observations were the classroom, class teacher and gender responsive pedagogy 100% scoring meant excellent classrooms and excellent teachers. Twelve classes were observed in the distribution of lower (1), middle (3) and upper class (6). The class excellence analyzed safety, cleanliness aura, arrangement, visuals, students work, learning areas and types of materials used. The excellence in the teacher was analyzed on class management, teacher attitude, question and answer peer learning strategy, independent feedback responsibility and student participation. Gender responsive pedagogy explored equity in interactions, request for tasks, peer learning, participation and feedback. The distribution of the percentage scores across classes and aspect are displayed in Figure 9.

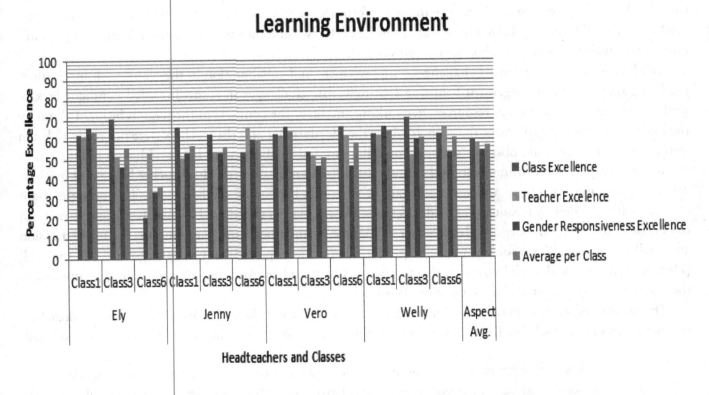

Figure 9 Learning Environment Excellence as a percentage in all aspects and classes

The learning environment brought out an above average on the scale of excellence. The class-, teacher-, and gender responsive- excellence all scored above mid-point (Figure 9). The respective averages for the three aspects were 69.44%, 58.07% and 54.44% respectively. The cumulative average of 58% of the expected 100% on excellence was observed.

Teams

Vero's team was at the performing stage predominantly. However she had in some instances been at forming, storming and norming stage. This outcome is in agreement with the teacher's outcome on teams. Hence the teams in Vero's school were at different stages. The teacher's perspective of the team based on Tuckman model showed that the school team was distributed in all stages of forming, storming, norming and performing. The schools were in transition and spread across the four stages. The performing stage was predominant; hence it shows that the levels of the teams were based on the members of the teams formed or the task given to the team. Vero's leadership tended to be almost horizontal. Welly's team leadership was highly horizontal. The teams in Welly's school were at different levels with most of them at the norming and forming stage according to Tuckman's model. The teams spent very little time at forming stage and rarely at the storming stage. Ely's teams were non – hierarchical as they were mostly horizontal. His lowest team leadership was his feeling of being left out in the information loop. Jenny's teams were in different groups depending on their tenure in the school. The long serving teachers were in the performing stage while the teachers with short tenure or new teachers were still norming. There was a clear grouping of the two and they were not homogenous. Jenny teams' horizontal capability is between horizontal and vertical.

The Headteachers experienced challenges, empowerment and collaboration in the teams with motivation, modeling support and management featuring sparingly. The challenges in teams included conflicts, lack of goal achievement, participation, resources, networking and bias. The conflicts in the schools brought about by the leadership structure. In one of the schools where the Headteacher and the teachers were not ready to listen to the deputy as they could observe "why are you telling us and the boss is not here and he has told us not to do this" Jenny, personal communication, February 2014. In another case the Headteacher being a union boss was usually away from school and was not aware of what was happening in the school. This brought about conflicts when the deputy Headteacher made decisions and the teacher called the Headteacher who contradicted the decision shared by the deputy Headteacher as she said "sometimes a teacher comes to me for permission and I tell this teacher "I am sorry you have to go during your own spare time, you can't go out, and they call [Headteacher] and he doesn't know that this teacher was in my office. And then he ends giving permission to the teacher". Jenny, personal communication, February 13, 2014.

The number of teachers in the school made conflicts inevitable but these were handled by the Headteachers and the deputies in the school. The Headteachers felt the teachers were not confident or did not feel empowered.

> "You know everybody is a decision maker, but there is a habit of teachers feeling that the Headteacher should be a small god and if one is having something they shy off sharing unless somebody motivates them to come forward and share. I don't want to call it fear but there is [an] assumptions that a Headteacher is a person who knows almost everything" Welly, personal communication, February 28, 2014.

Lack of commitment in the school activities were some of the issues raised by the Headteachers. Decision making also involved the Headteachers who realized that decision making process was also a learning opportunity for them. The indecision of conflicts from decision were observed when "Sometimes the decision made is not auguring well with the staff and the students, I am forced to go back to the drawing board and rethink and come out with a different thing Jenny, personal communication February 13, 2014.. Jane noted that

> Some are correct some are ….. It is food for thought [whereby] you sit down and check whether this is the right decision. I should have done it the other way. The other way round,

I'm not saying whatever decisions we are making are 100% good. Some of them are even totally negative but after the impact is when you realize this is not the decision we should have made. We should have gone the other way. Jenny, personal communication, February 13, 2014.

Indecisiveness or lack of participation in decision making indicated lack of empowerment or commitment. However, the experiences of the decision making process was a learning experience for the Headteachers. Failure of achieving goals was another issue of challenges in the team. As the Headteacher explained that

We set goals all the time. Not all the time the set goals are achieved. I try as much as I can [to] achieve my set goals, but sometimes it's impossible. Not to the fullest. At a certain point we somehow achieve some goals but not all of them. Not all the goals.

Jenny, personal communication, February 13, 2014.

The Headteachers appreciated some of the challenges that they experienced

Participation was expressed through sharing, cooperation and collaboration which happened within teams. The Headteacher and the teams collectively set goals, mission and vision at the beginning of the year. Participation in the team was a challenge as teachers were not forthcoming to take up responsibilities. The Headteacher had to appoint people. Moreover, the Headteacher needed to identify those who were dragging others behind and offer close supervision. Power issues influenced the level of participation as others just did for the purpose of being seen "The teachers did not feel empowered and shy off from participation as observed" Welly personal communication, March, 3 2014.

The Headteacher felt powerless due to influential external interferences. The Headteachers shared that

As a...ok let me say as a leader, I treat all my teachers equally. But as perception as per society, there are some who are special and they are beyond my control. Yeah. I have such teachers here. Even if I want to make a decision on equal terms...even if I make it. Let's say I use my powers I say this is how things are going to be, there is always a...that's why I use the words "attitude" and "barrier". I have bosses who can intervene and they kind of assist these particular teachers. Jenny, personal communication, February 5, 2014.

The Headteachers embraced the aspect of networking which was part of the topics in the ELMT. The Headteachers noted that "I am becoming old I had tried earlier to mobilize nearby schools like Zimlat so that we can come together have Zimlat which is a private school, Nyamteka and Shimo la tewa. I wish we could work together with them, it's the pipeline" Welly, personal communication, February 28, 2014.

Although they were inspired "I always aspire to work with neighbors but due to busy schedule am not able" Ely, personal communication, February 27, 2014. There still were challenges. The Headteachers consulted fellow heads where they needed assistance.

There was a level of empowerment among the teams as delegation ran through all activities. There was a belief in all members and the Headteacher delegated duties to subject panel heads and respected their decisions and where panels were nonexistence the Headteacher set them up. The delegation was based on the teacher interest hence allowing them to perform the delegated tasks. The Headteachers went to the extent of sending the teachers to represent then in external meetings.

Resources both time and physical were part of the challenges. One example was that ICT was lacking in their schools. The other was time as they said "yeah we always set a time limit but meeting it is the problem. Meeting the time which we er… Jenny, personal communication, February 5, 2014.

Collaboration in teams was evident through activities, consultations, participation, target settings and tasks. School activities brought up the members of the team as the head noted "We have a get together at the end of the term, prize giving day in school, we interact with others through athletics" Vero, personal communication, February 6, 2014.

The teams were motivated when the motivation came from incentives, encouragement and role modeling. The members were given tokens for the good work that they had done. The recognition allowed the teachers to work together to improve the results which was a measure of performance. Parents were also involved in contribution for the recognition of the teachers work. This brought a holistic view on incentives with all the stakeholders of parents and management involved. Another form of incentives was encouragement as the Headteachers shared "I encouraged our teachers to be one through welfare and meetings. I have an open door office and if something goes wrong they are free to come to me and we discuss and look for solutions". Ely, personal communication, February, 27, 2014.

The teachers are encouraged by the Headteachers to be committed and to deliver in terms of learning outcomes. Beyond incentives and encouragement the Headteachers walked the talk by role modeling. The activities decided by the team were modeled by the Headteachers and this inspired the teachers as noted. "If the Headteacher is coming to school early who am I not to follow such" Welly, personal communication, February 28, 2014.

Finally the teams were supported through priority setting and continuous professional learning. The teams will sit together with the Headteachers to set priorities on what to work on. The involvement of the teacher in priority setting allowed the teachers to undertake professional learning opportunities. The Headteachers gave the teachers permission to attend professional learning sessions as well as practice what they had learnt from the sessions.

The type of teams in the schools indicated the type of leadership by the Headteachers. The teams in the school were at different stages based on the tasks and the length of interaction. Similarly the team leadership was mainly horizontal with only one Headteacher leadership lying between horizontal and vertical. The Headteacher expressed challenges in empowerment and collaboration in teams with motivation, modeling support and management featuring sparingly. The Headteacher used several approaches to overcome challenges in the teams. Some of the approaches were motivation, encouragement and priority setting

Networking

Networking is a key aspect in the ELMT sessions. The study explored the involvement of the government and the BOM and PTA in the school governance. The Headteachers and teachers had different perspectives on the roles of BOM and PTA and government respectively. The perspectives were either divergent or convergent depending on different aspects or foci.

Headteachers perspective on networking

The Headteachers saw networking from BOM, PTA and the government addressing four aspects which included quality assurance, helping management, and support and conflict management. The main role of the government was for quality assurance to the Headteachers. Although there were no frequent visits at least the school had routine inspection twice a year. The Headteachers regarded the government as function of inspection. The school visits included classrooms observation, analysis of administration records and engaging with the students. The school inspection then gave individual feedback through dialogue by providing strength followed by weakness and proposed remedy. The inspector then assembled the whole school and interacted with them sharing on how to improve teaching and improve performance. The Headteachers are first school inspectors and this response presented some support from the Headteachers for quality assurance. However the low frequency meant that the Headteachers had to utilize their quality assurance skills shared during ELMT.

The Headteachers felt that the BOM and PTA had a crucial responsibility in the school governance. According to the Headteachers the BOM and PTA was responsible for parental involvement. They were responsible for convincing parents about their roles and how to take responsibility for their children's learning at school. There were many situations where parents were illiterate and could not sign the students' diary. The BOM and PTA were responsible in assisting such parents to be involved in their children's learning. Sometimes it was worse as parents were not aware of their children's examination as noted "that is a problem in fact I have being surprised, somebody comes to pay for KCPE registration fee when you ask him how many marks your child got promoted to class 8, the parent says the child does not show me his report book" Welly, personal communication, March 3, 2014. There was recognition of the responsibility the BOM and PTA and there was disappointed on the level of responsibility. The Headteachers were aware felt the need for there to be school partners in school governance. Managing conflicts by the Headteachers for BOM and PTA came in two formats. One was for them to manage the conflicts in cases where there arose behavior sponsors (churches and mosques) and other involved bodies. The other conflict that the Headteachers struggled with was to get the BOM and PTA to be involved in the school activities. The resolution of conflicts and the involvement of the BOM and PTA was a challenge in itself. The BOM and PTA had a responsibility of working with the Headteachers and planning how to conduct school matters. The BOM and PTA were responsible in weighing issues and prioritizing them through frequent meetings. On the down side the Headteachers felt that three meetings per school term as required was not enough. According to some Headteachers the BOM and PTA were irresponsible as they did not have influence or power. The Headteachers were disappointed with such situations wishing for a strong BOM and PTA to influence the teachers; in such situation the Headteachers took the lead to guide the BOM and PTA members.

The Headteachers identified support from both government and the BOM and PTA. the support for BOM and PTA in discipline, motivation standards and supporting students to study at home. The BOM and PTA were also supportive on infrastructure such as bookstores, furniture, roofs and toilets. The BOM and PTA helped in supervision of construction and purchase. The government supported FPE by supplying funds as well as supporting content coverage. The downside was where support lacked or was not 100% or not good.

The Headteachers identified networking with BOM, PTA and government as responding to quality assurance, management support and conflict management.

Teachers' perspective on networking

The teachers apparently did not know the BOM and PTA members and when they knew them they complained of low level of education and not supporting school or student learning. Their main discontent was the BOM and PTA monolithic focus of NEP. The involvement of the government was seen by the teachers as quality assurance and provision or supporting professional development. The teachers had a different perspective regarding the BOM and PTA. They knew the requirement of the BOM and PTA and their roles in the school. However they did not know the BOM and PTA members. Knowing the BOM and PTA roles brought out aspects which had not been realized by the BOM and PTA. The teachers expressed their disappointments on the level of education of the BOM and PTA members and their lack or low performance in their role in supporting the school. The teachers felt that the BOM and PTA focused their effect on the examination exit classes and ignored the other classes.

The government (managers) involvement was noted by the teachers. They observed that the key role was quality assurance and professional development. The teachers decried on the numbers of teachers and wanted the government to employ more. The support by the government on the schools' development plan process was observed by the teachers. However the teachers felt that the government should play a key role in situation of sponsored school as infighting has impacted on the schools development.

The teachers had a different perspective on BOM and PTA. They knew their roles and felt that BOM and PTA did. The teachers were disappointed with BOM's and PTA's level of education. The teachers considered the government as supportive but decried on the numbers of teachers in the schools and the support they got from the government in terms of sponsorship.

Skills transferred to school governance from the ELMT

After reviewing the leadership, teams and networking the next level of inquiry was to determine the level of implementation through open ended inquiry and course content guided questions. The implementation of the skills was done in three levels. In the first level, teachers in the school were interviewed to understand how they experienced the Headteachers leadership. This was used to triangulate with the responses from the two other levels. In the second level the Headteachers were asked without guidance of the aspect which they have been implementing after the ELMT training skills. Two thirds of what the Headteachers implemented managing resources, leadership and pedagogical leadership equally. A third of the responses covered action research, emerging issues, guidance and counseling, reflective practice and networking in that order. A key concept missing in the pre-guided responses was evaluation. In the third level the Headteachers were given guidance with the list of the topics and asked for the definition of the topics with examples and the implementation of the topics with examples. According to the Headteachers' perspective, their understanding of the ELM topics ranged between fair and good. No Headteacher had an excellent understanding of any of the ELM topics. The response options were weighted against the contact time of the topics. The responses according to the weighting indicated a 55% understanding of the ELM topics. A similar approach was done to the frequency of implementation which ranged from never to always. The responded frequency of implementation ranged from rare, occasionally to always with the latter two representing 98% of the responses. This showed that most of the implementations were in the categories of occasionally and always at equal levels. The implemented aspects were analyzed against the weightings and the outcome indicated a 55% implementation of all the aspects exposed to the Headteachers. Although the percentages on understanding and implementation were similar the distribution between fair and good and occasionally and always were not similar.

The level of implementation was linked to the level of understanding the concepts. Two thirds of the implementation was in the topics of managing resources, leadership and pedagogical leadership equally implemented. The other third was action research, emerging issues, guidance and counseling, reflective practice and networking in that order in order of understanding and frequency of implementation. The understanding of the topics was between fair and good. The frequency of implementation was mainly occasionally and always at equal levels. The weightage of the topics resulted to 55% percentage level of understanding and 55% level of implementation. There percentages were similar cumulatively but there was not congruency on the responses between understanding (fair and good) and implementation (always and occasionally). Cumulatively there was an alignment between the levels of understanding and implementation.

Headteachers perspectives on identified barriers

Headteachers perspective on barriers was explored on action before, during and after training (Broad, 2002; Broad & Newstrom, 1992), ranking the barriers identified by Newstrom's, categorizing their impacts (Newstrom, 1986), identifying perspective on Coates organizational barriers (Coates, 2007) and identifying Headteachers' barriers.

Actions at different stages of training

Earlier Broad & Newstrom (1992) and later Broad (2002) identified actions which should be done during different stages of training for effective transfer of the training skills. The Headteachers were required to share the frequency of the Broad and Newstrom's actions that they do at different stages of the training. The type of activities done frequently at different stages of the training will influence the transfer of ELMT skills to school governance. On all the cases the frequency ranged from occasionally to always. Seldom and almost did not feature in any of the responses.

Before the training

Broad and Newstrom's identified actions before the ELMT training fell in three categories of always, frequently and occasionally (Table 10)

During the training

During the training the frequency of attendance was always as this was mandatory and three absences meant being struck off the register. The other Broad and Newstrom's actions were either occasionally or frequently (Table 11).

After The Training

After the training the Broad and Newstrom's actions were either frequently done or always done (Table 12)

Table 10 *Frequency of actions by the Headteachers before ELMT*

Responded as Always Actions	Responded as Frequent Actions	Responded as Occasional Action
Ward off negative pre-course feedback	Participate in advance activities	Develop questions for trainer
Arrive at course early, well rested	Talk about your upcoming learning program with key managers	Research other related material
Discuss the change with manager to understand expectations.	Review objectives and expectations with managers	Clarify location, time and dress code
Note one's own performance gap		Clear up daily activities prior to the learning program
Prepare personal objectives - why am I going?	Write personal goals	Actively explore all learning options
Read up on the topic, talk to trainer and complete pre-work	Delegate duties that cannot be taken care of prior to the learning program	Bring appropriate equipment and materials to the program
Sort out personal responsibilities that could interfere with program	Go to program with clear and open mind	Identify a specific job situation that can be used as an example
Take the course when you need to use it (just in time)		Provide input into program planning
Ensure learning is part of your development plan		
Understand what is expected after the course.		

Table 11 *Actions by the Headteachers during ELMT*

Frequently	Occasionally
Focus on learning and reduce distractions	
Maintain an "Ideas and Applications" notebook	
Participate actively and ask questions	
Think about how to apply learning back on job	
Try to personalize learning to meet needs	
receive feedback, reinforce learning	
Ask/give workplace examples	
Be open-minded and set aside paradigms where necessary	
Collaborate with trainer over agenda	
Create a course outline to pass on at work	
Develop plans on how to:	Link with a buddy
Apply learning	Pay close attention – listen
Form support groups	Understand.
Anticipate relapse	Make notes on key points
Create behavioral contracts	
Enjoy the learning process – have fun	
Learn/apply/share	

Table 12 *Frequency of Newstrom's actions after ELMT*

Always	Frequently
Develop job aids	
Provide honest, targeted feedback to trainer	Practice self-management
Seek manager's support to implement any change of strategies	Practice, practice, practice
Develop a mentoring relationship	Discuss performance objectives and action plans with manager
Get others involved and share learning principles	Review learning content and learned skills with manager
Look for behavioral change.	Schedule follow-up with trainer.
Maintain contact with new network	Write summary of learning
Turn learning principles into a project	
Develop short term/long term plans.	
Participate in refresher courses.	
Present findings to peers.	

Headteachers ranking and categorizing impact of Newstrom's Barriers.

The barriers were explored based on Newstrom's barriers. The exploration included ranking and the impact of the identified barriers at different points of the training. The ranking by the Headteachers differed with Newstrom's findings Table 13.

Table 13 Transfer of training ranking by the Headteachers (HT) Compare to Newstrom's ranking

HT's Ranking	Newstrom's Ranking	Barriers
4	1	Lack of reinforcement on the job
5	2	Interference from immediate environment (work, time pressures, insufficient authority, ineffective work processes, inadequate equipment and facilities).
6	3	Non-supportive organizational culture (no strong philosophical support for the goals of professional development programs).
2	4	Trainees' perception of impractical training programs.
8	5	Trainees' perception of irrelevant training content.
3	6	Trainees' discomfort with change and associated effort (undue discomfort or extra effort).
9	7	Separation from inspiration or support of the trainer.
7	8	Trainees' perception of poorly designed/delivered training.
1	9	Pressure from peers to resist changes (not transfer training to the workplace).

Note From "Leveraging Management Development through the Management of Transfer". By J. W. Newstrom, 1986, *Journal of Management Development*, 5(5), 33 – 45

Newstrom had ranked the barriers into two categories of greatest barriers (1, 2 and 3) and least barriers (4, 5, 6 and 8). If the ranking is reviewed in three categories of great (1, 2, 3), mild (4, 5, 6) and least (7, 8, 9) there were some alignment in the least barriers 9 and 7 both falling in the least categories for both the Headteachers' ranking and Newstrom's ranking. There was a swop between the Headteachers and Newstrom's barriers. What the Headteachers considered as mild impact barriers were actually Newstrom's great impact barriers. The outlier was the pressure from peers which was greatest impact barriers for the Headteachers yet least impact barriers from Newstrom's findings.

The Headteachers ranked Newstrom's barriers which were compared with Newstrom's ranking. The comparison showed mixed relationships. There was a flip on the ranking where Newstrom's great impact ranking were Headteacher's mild impact ranking. The least barriers had similar ranking. There was one outlier which was considered as great impact by Newstrom's but the Headteachers ranked it as the least barrier.

The impact of the barriers at different stages of ELMT was also compared with Newstrom's findings. The comparisons varied on different aspects (Table 14).

Table 14 *Headteachers' (HT) perspective on the impact of barriers compared with Newstrom (N's) findings*

Before		During		After		Barriers
HT	N's	HT	N's	HT	N's	
1		2		2	1	Lack of reinforcement on the job.
1		1	2	2	1	Interference from immediate environment (work, time pressures, insufficient authority, ineffective work processes, inadequate equipment and facilities).
1	1	1	2	2	2	Non-supportive organizational culture (no strong philosophical support for the goals of professional development programs).
2		2	1	2		Trainees' perception of impractical training programs.
2		1	1	2		Trainees' perception of irrelevant training content.
2	2	2	2	2	1	Trainees' discomfort with change and associated effort (undue discomfort or extra effort).
2		2		2	1	Separation from inspiration or support of the trainer.
1		1	1	2		Trainees' perception of poorly designed/delivered training.
1	2	1		1	1	Pressure from peers to resist changes (not transfer training to the workplace).

1= Primary time impact 2=secondary time impact

Note From "Leveraging Management Development through the Management of Transfer". By J. W. Newstrom, 1986, *Journal of Management Development*, 5(5), 33 – 45

Before the training non-supportive organizational culture and trainee discomfort with change were perceived similar to Newstrom's findings. Pressure from peers was perceived as primary and secondary for Headteachers and Newstrom's findings respectively. Lack of reinforcement on the job and interference from immediate environment were primary time impact by the Headteachers while they were uncategorized by Newstrom findings. Other unranked aspects were trainee's perception of poorly designed or delivered training, separation from inspiration of the trainer, trainees' perception of irrelevant training content and trainees' perception of impractical training programs were which secondary impact according to the Headteachers.

Most of the barriers during the training were categorized. Three barriers uncategorized by Newstrom's but categorized by the Headteachers were pressure from peers to resist changes (primary), separation from inspiration or support of the trainer (secondary) and lack on reinforcement on the job (secondary). Similarities were in trainees' perception of poorly designed/delivered training and trainees' perception of irrelevant training content (primary) and trainees' discomfort with change and associated effort (secondary). The three barriers of trainees' perception of impractical training programs, interference from immediate environment and non-supportive organizational culture alternated between primary and secondary impact for the Headteachers and Newstrom's findings.

After the training unranked Newstrom's barriers of trainees' perception of impractical training programs, trainees' perception of irrelevant training content and trainees' perception of poorly designed/delivered training received a secondary impact by the Headteachers. Non-supportive organizational culture received a secondary impact while pressure from peers to resist changes received a primary impact for both Headteachers and Newstrom's findings.

Separation from inspiration or support of the trainer, trainees' discomfort with change and associated effort, interference from immediate environment and lack of reinforcement on the job were all categorized as secondary impact by the Headteachers while Newstrom's finding categorized them as primary impact.

Newstrom's barriers were categorized to have impacts either as primary or secondary. Newstrom impacts varied based on the timeline of before, during and after EMLT. The Headteachers categorized the impact of the barriers and the Headteachers categorization was compared with Newstrom's categories. Before the training there were two barriers which were categorized as primary for both Headteachers and Newstrom's categorization. One barrier was flipped on impact. Newstrom's uncategorized barriers were seen as primary (2 barriers) and Secondary (4 barriers). During the training Newstrom's uncategorized barriers were categorized by Headteachers as primary impact (1 barrier) and secondary impact (2 barriers). 2 categorized barriers were similar to Headteachers and Newstrom's categories. 3 barriers alternated between primary and secondary impact for the Headteachers and Newstrom's categories. After the training Newstrom's uncategorized barriers were considered by the Headteachers as having secondary impact. 2 barriers had similar impact for both the Headteacher and Newstrom. 4 barriers flipped in categories as Headteachers found them as having secondary impact while Newstrom categorized them as having primary impact.

Headteachers perspectives on organization barriers to trainer transfer

Organization behavior can be a support or a hindrance to the transfer of ELMT skills in the schools. The Headteachers were asked to gauge organizational support for performance improvement as well as to identify the behavioral model the organization prefers to operate in.

Headteachers' perspectives on organizational support for performance improvement

To explore how well the organizational systems supported the Headteachers' efforts to improve performance, the Headteachers were given a set of statements where they were supposed to respond to the level of agreement with Coates (2007) statements. The Headteachers strongly agreed on all statements that they were given as indicated in Table 15.

The Headteachers strongly agreed on all the statements given by Coates (2007). The statement referred to the organizational support which influenced performance improvement.

Table 15 Coates *Strongly agreed statements by the Headteachers on efforts to improve performance.*

Coates Statements
My job responsibilities require me to use the skills and concepts I learned in training.
Additional learning resources such as programs, videos, and books are available to help me improve how I perform the skills and concepts I learned in training.
I have regular opportunities to learn from others, to talk with co – workers program participants, or mentors about "lessons learned" related to the skills and concepts I learned in training.
I receive feedback from surveys that measure how much I've improved the way I perform the skills and concepts I learned in training.
I've been given assignments or tasks with opportunities to apply the skills and concepts I learned in training.
Management has made it clear that I'm expected to use the skills and concepts I learned in training.
My department structure makes it easy for me to apply skills and concepts I learned in training.
My manager has told me that I'll be held accountable for using the skills and concepts I learned in training.
My manager is actively involved in my ongoing learning and development related to the skills and concepts I learned in training.
My manager sets a good example for using the skills and concepts I learned in training.
My organization gives me adequate support to help me improve the skills and concepts I learned in training.
My organization's policies and practices encourage me apply the skills and concepts I learned in training.
My performance goals and objectives require me to use the skills and concepts I learned in training.
My performance review evaluates how well I'm using the skills and concepts I learned in training.
The rewards and incentives available to me to motivate me to use the skills and concepts I learned in training.

Note From *"Enhance the training of training: Tips, Tools and Intelligence for Trainers", By D. E* Coates, 2007. *0710*. (J. Brusino, Ed.) USA: ASTD. Pg 10.

Organization preference of behavioral model

The Headteachers were required to identify the model of the organization they will prefer to operate in. From the statement given the Headteachers were to indicate how rarely the school displayed the described behavior. Two extremes stood out as the Headteacher selected either almost never or almost always. According to the Headteachers the management expected the teachers to give more than minimal performance. The Headteachers acknowledged that in all circumstances the teachers did not leave the school because it provides a lot of security and the management's main concern was to improve the NEP. The other preferred behaviors were either frequently or occasionally (Table 16).

The preferred organizational behavioral model was further analyzed to establish whether the organizational behavioral model was among autocratic, custodial, supportive and collegial (Clark, 2013). Analysis of the organization behavior brought out the predominant behavior of the schools. All the schools apart from one operated predominantly on a supportive mode. According to Clark (2013) Supportive mode is an approach that depends upon leadership invested on money or power. Through leadership the school helps leaders to grow and accomplish things in the school. The school that was not predominant supportive was predominant custodial. In the custodial mode is where paternalism is practice. According to Clark, the school depends on economic resources to meet the security needs of its teacher which leads to dependence upon the school. The other dominant mode was collegial mode which is a team concept that depends upon the management building partnership with the teacher.

The preferred school behavioral modes were in three categories. All the schools apart from one operated predominantly on a supportive mode which was leadership invested upon power. The school that was not predominant supportive was predominant custodial where paternalism was in practice. The other dominant mode was collegial mode which is a team concept that depends upon the management building partnership with the teacher.

The preferred school behavioral modes were in three categories. All the schools apart from one operated predominantly on a supportive mode which was leadership invested upon power. The school that was not predominant supportive was predominant custodial where paternalism was in practice. The other dominant mode was collegial mode which is a team concept that depends upon the management building partnership with the teacher.

Table 16 *Most of the preferred organization behavioral model the Headteachers prefer to operate in.*

Occasionally	Frequently
There is a partnership between Headteachers and teachers.	Both managers and teachers want to create better job performance.
Most of the teachers seem content with their position.	Teachers are part of the decision making process.
Things get accomplished around here because teachers fear for their jobs.	The managers display real leadership traits and are respected by the teachers.
Although the teachers have good benefits, they tend to give only minimal performance.	There is a real feeling of teamwork.
	Although the teachers are happy and contented, they give only passive cooperation.
Most of the jobs are considered "minimum wage" jobs.	The teachers feel they are part of the organization.
Although people obey their leaders, they do not respect the leaders.	The teachers feel a real responsibility to make things work.
The teachers 'main concern is for the security of their families and themselves.	When things go wrong, the main concern is to fix it, not to lay blame.
Only Headteachers are allowed to make decisions.	Things happen around here because of the self-discipline of every teacher.
The teachers 'main concern is to provide for their families and themselves.	There is enthusiasm among the teachers to better job performance.
	The teachers feel they are recognized for their work.
	The teachers feel their jobs hold high esteem and are of great value to the organization.

Note The statement From "The Art and Science of Leadership", By D. Clark, 2013 categorized according the respondents responses

Headteacher's experienced barriers

The Headteachers identified several barriers some of which were unique to respective schools while others were generic across the four schools on their transfer of ELMT skills to school governance. The main barriers were teachers and resources which were inhibiting the transfer of ELMT skills. Other barriers of which emerged with lesser prominent but with equal distribution were culture/emerging issues, stakeholders (parents), teams, and policy

Teachers were the main stumbling block for the transfer if training skill in the school governance. The issues with teachers included attitude, change, commitment, delegation, economic, parents, resistance, resources, role modeling, and sensitization team work.

The Headteachers were coming back to school with new approaches to teaching learning and assessment. However the teachers had a belief of traditional approach to the teaching practice so the belief system was a hindrance to the teacher to take up the new approaches. The attitudes were also inhibited to the teacher's profession where some believed they were teachers by accident the Headteachers observed "being a teacher is in fact associated to some of them like a curse.... Some don't even introduce themselves as teachers they will rather say nothing. They have associated the profession with failure" (Interviews 3 Jane 13 February 2014). Attitude posed a challenge to the transfer of ELMT skills by the Headteachers. Opposing actions like rigidity to change, resistance, lack of commitment formed formidable barriers to transfer of ELMT skills. The teachers were rigid to change and it was difficult for them to embrace the new approaches introduced by the Headteachers. The teachers were also resistant to what was being introduced. Newstrom (1986) had identified the barrier of discomfort with change and associated effort. The teachers were comfortable with the status quo and when the Headteachers changed work practices the teachers were reluctant and tried to push the blame to the students. The Headteachers shared that teachers were shying off from their tasks or duties showing lack of commitment. During ELMT the Headteachers undertook action research and one of the Headteachers cited lack of respondents while undertaking the action research on punctuality. Other areas of lack of commitment were ending lessons early, arriving to lessons late and not undertaking remedial lessons. Staff absenteeism was also an issue and a similar observation was made nationally by the TSC and MOEST. Absenteeism meant time utility was a barrier as teacher did not finish the syllabus due to time. Lack of commitment was a hindrance as the teachers could not take up the new approaches. The Headteachers were trying to stir commitment and allow the teachers to perform well in their work. Freedom to interact, confidence and economic status posed a barrier to the Headteachers' ELMT skills transfer. In most of the schools the teachers and students had no freedom with the parents locking away one crucial stakeholder during the induction. The Headteachers and the teachers lack freedom to interact among themselves and with the students. The skilled Headteachers tried to empower their teachers after the ELMT; however the teachers lacked confidence to take up the new responsibilities and kept on referring to the Headteachers. The lack of confidence in teachers challenge the coaching or mentoring the Headteachers were trying to implement to empower the teachers. However, conflicting interests were on the way such as economic status. The teachers were not willing to do an extra work (remedial) or come on weekends because they wanted to make an extra shilling. The teachers preferred to do other economic activities or take tuition out of school to gain extra money to sustain them economically. The Headteachers had no way of economical supplement as the teachers are paid through the TSC. Despite the Headteachers trying to role model, the teachers did not take up what the Headteachers were role modeling. Sensitization was very low and the Headteachers remained alone trying to do things differently while the teachers watched and continued with how they used to work before the Headteachers attended ELMT. The team aspect among the teacher was an issue. Cooperation among the teachers was wanting as competition reigned due to the brown envelope offered after improving the mean score. Moreover the Headteachers experienced team building challenges as they tried to encourage female teachers. These were most of the barriers and they were brought about by the teachers. The teachers being the majority meant the Headteachers was facing multiple barriers from the people who were required to work closely with them. The Headteachers struggled with these barriers.

Resources posed a barrier to Headteachers ELMT transfer of skills. All aspects of resources physical, time and financial posed barriers. The physical resources were those linked to the innovative approaches being introduced by the Headteachers. There were limited resources for development and implementation, some schools had one toilet for one hundred students, there was no school fence and some of the books were outdated. Time was a major barrier as the sharing, presentation of the new approaches required time, and furthermore the teaching in the ways also required more planning time whereas the teachers were struggling with time management, this did not seem to be transferred to the teachers. The final barrier was the resources. The preparation of the Headteachers required them to utilize resources to enhance school governance. Despite the government giving FPE money of 1032 shillings per student per year, the Headteachers felt that this was not enough to cater for the needs. The Headteachers resolved to work with what they had.

Culture of the school was a key barrier. Teachers were comfortable with the status quo and were not ready to take risks and try out new approaches. The status quo aspects of lack of reading culture, low or non-reflective practices and external interference of the schools aspects that aimed to be eradicated by ELMT posed a formidable barrier. Although the Headteachers were prepared to handle emerging issues, the issues also posed a barrier to the ELMT transfer of skills. This is because the issues were dynamic, contextual related and in some cases seasonal. Such issues included drugs, teenage pregnancies, early marriages, child labor, abusive parents, and prostitution among others. Despite the Headteachers being exposed to some of the emerging issues the dynamic nature and forms of the emerging issues presented a challenge for the Headteachers. One solution or approach was not applicable to all.

The Headteachers cited policy as a barrier. This included schools which belonged to church or communities and were taken by the government and now the former owners wanted them back. There were court cases and this disrupted the transfer of skills. This was limited to two schools which were under that condition. Policy on discipline was also a hindrance as it was not aligned to what the Headteachers were exposed to in terms of addressing disciplines in schools. Coates (2007) has identified policy structure as influencing a statement which the Headteachers strongly agreed with.

The inclusion of all stakeholders in learning was one aspect of the ELMT. The Headteachers tried their best but the barriers proved insurmountable due to lack of bandwidth and support from all the stakeholders. One of the stakeholders were the parents and the lack of support which formed a barrier was non- attendance of meeting, lack of financial support to the school and their non – involvement in the students learning. With support missing from such a key stakeholder, the Headteachers faced a barrier including the involvement of stakeholders in the school. Students as the focus in the school also brought up barrier. The barriers were financial and time management. These two had a dual relationship. The students were doing menial jobs such as scrap metal selling among others because they wanted to make money instead of attending lessons. After getting their money they wanted to spend on PlayStations instead of learning, this meant attendance and punctuality in school was affected and hence the management of the student was a challenge.

The main barriers were teachers and resources which were inhibiting the transfer of ELMT skills. Other barriers of which emerged with lesser prominent but with equal distribution were culture/emerging issues, stakeholders (parents), teams, and policy. Teachers were the main stumbling block for the transfer of training skill in the school governance. The issues with teachers included attitude, change, commitment, delegation, economic, parents, resistance, resources, role modeling, and sensitization team work. Resources posed a barrier to Headteachers ELMT transfer of skills. All aspects of resources physical, time and financial posed barriers. The physical resources were those linked to the innovative approaches being introduced by the Headteachers. Culture of the school was a key barrier. Teachers were comfortable with the status quo and were not ready to take risks and try out new approaches.

How Headteachers overcome the barriers during ELMT skills transfer

The Headteachers were asked open ended questions to explore how they managed the barriers faced during ELMT skills transfer. Several themes came up with managers and stakeholder support taking the most prominence. Other aspects included appreciating change, fear (information provided before the training, networking and empowerment), and participation during training, teamwork, managing resources and motivation.

The school managers namely TSC and MoEST played key roles in overcoming the barriers in the transfer of ELMT skills to school governance. The two managers wanted teachers to attend ELMT. This was empowering the Headteachers. A memorandum of understanding between AKAM and the two managers ensured that the transfers of the trained teachers from the schools were minimal. Lack of transfer gave the Headteachers the tenure to implement ELMT their stations the managers also requested the Headteachers to share their ELMT course outline. The Headteachers saw this as a way of allowing them to transfer their skills because their managers knew what they were learning. The Headteachers categorized Newstrom action of seeking managers' support as always after ELMT. In some instances the managers told the Headteachers "I will be coming to your school to see how you are implementing performance management" Interview 3 Jane 13 February 2014. Furthermore support came with the TSC and MOEST offering supplementary / complimentary training and allowing either the Headteachers to attend or to send their teachers. The ability for the Headteachers to appreciate the complimentary or supplementary of these workshops allowed the Headteachers to feel supported. The Headteachers involved the education officials who were aware of the content and had authority of the teachers involved in the transfer of ELMT skills.

To overcome the barriers the Headteachers cited support from different sectors. Their main support was from the stakeholders. Others included mechanisms and amount of support, professional learning opportunities and action research. Support was the main aspect that the Headteachers cited as helping them overcome the barriers in the transfer of ELMT skills to school governance. The support mechanism after the course made my concepts to widen (Interview 3 Welly 3 March 2014). The Headteachers cited support from parents; this was congruent to other responses. Some of the innovations included resources, Headteachers requested and received support from the politicians (members of parliament and county assemblies) and parents in implementing resource based innovations. This involvement of the managers was supported in overcoming some of the barriers that involved human resource or were systemic. Furthermore the involvement of local administration such as village elders and chiefs allowed the Headteachers to address the barriers such as emerging issues, early pregnancies, marriages, and drugs. Sponsors such as churches and mosques also reached out to support where applicable. Apart from networking, stakeholders involved were also used to support and overcome the barriers. The stakeholders provided incentives, support and worked together. Parents were asked to provide incentives to the teachers. Parents were also required to support teaching, learning and assessment, remedial teaching and hardworking teachers. The parents were encouraged to care for the school. There were attempts to create structures such that the BOM, parents and students were working together. The stakeholder's involvement supplemented the networking initiatives hence a motivation on the barriers identified. Another unique support element was action research. The Headteachers observed that by undertaking action research they did two things that is, implementing what they had learnt and learning from the implementations. This offered a unique support to the Headteachers. The Headteachers categorically agreed though the support was not 100/% they had support above 50/%. The fact of being aware that you are not alone in the transfer of skills encourages the Headteachers and influences their transfer of ELMT skills to school governance.

The Headteachers were coming up with innovative ways of governing schools after ELMT having gone through exposure to possibilities of change. Apart from the Headteacher, the school had many teachers who were expected to appreciate change and embrace it. The same appreciation should be embraced by Headteachers as they introduce innovations so as to improve NEP trends. The Headteacher appreciated change and tried to influence the teachers to take up change.

Fear was an element that could be managed to overcome the barriers. When the Headteachers enrolled in an ELMT course some were joining after an extensive time in school governance. Joining ELMT challenged what they had been doing for many years. Their experiences and the struggle to complete ELMT created fear of implementation. The Headteachers cited that the fear could be overcome by the information of ELMT being provided in digital including level of encouragement and tasks before ELMT. Apart from information, networking with colleagues from the same cohort bridged over the barriers. The Headteachers learnt from the peer experiences of their colleagues as they governed the schools in new ways. In the action after ELMT the Headteachers had noted that they were always maintaining contact with new network, presenting findings to their peers and getting others involved and sharing their learning (Newstrom, 2008). Furthermore the Headteachers has strongly agreed on "I have regular opportunities to learn from others, to talk with co – workers program participants, or mentors about "lessons learned" related to the skills and concepts I learned in training" (Coates, 2007). The Headteachers sought to work with others through networking. The Headteachers acknowledged they would not be able to overcome the barriers single handedly and they involved other Headteachers, education officers, ELMT facilitates and like-minded teachers. The Headteachers reached out to their peers to find out how they were implementing their ELMT, this allowed them to have some ideas on how to handle the barriers they were facing. Consultations with the ELMT facilitators allowed the Headteachers to navigate through some of the barriers. The key aspect of networking was involvement of like-minded teachers or teachers who embraced change. The Headteachers involved such teachers and empowered them to take the lead in initiating and implementing the innovations. Inclusion by reaching out to others formed a network framework which supported the Headteachers to overcome the barriers they had identified.

Participating in the training was one thing the Headteachers cited as a way of overcoming the barriers, according to the Headteachers the practical and hands on experiences during the training gave them opportunity to understand concepts in a peer environment. The Headteachers noted that during ELMT they had opportunity to guide, dictate or influence how they wanted to learn as well as what they wanted to learn. This gave the Headteachers confidence as the ELMT was responding to their needs. They developed a positive attitude to the ELMT which could influence their transfer of ELMT skills to school governance.

The Headteachers realized the importance of forming teams among teachers, parents and students within the team's consultations and advice seeking was natured. Dialogue was encouraged in the teams and the team members freely expressed their views. The dialogue allowed reflective practice among the members allowing them to learn from the innovative approaches they were implementing. The team allowed a group of people to try out innovations in a safe and friendly peer environment.

Another aspect that enabled the Headteachers to overcome barriers during the ELMT skill transfer was the management of resources. This began by the resource mobilization through fund raising, donor sensitization and exploration of local, low cost, no cost resources. This was followed by allocation and utility of the limited resources. The Headteachers did operational analysis to ensure maximum effective utility of the limited resources. Resources a key ingredient to school governance was addressed through provision, utility and managing.

The Headteachers identified motivation as a basic need with multiple returns. They began the motivation by provision of basics like tea and lunch which allowed the teachers to stay in school and enhanced productivity. The Headteachers also identified the hot spots and they ensured them nurtured and supported such teachers in the hot spots. Headteachers observed that "I make sure the ones who are supportive, I also give full support and when the others see that there is something good coming unaona mmoja mmoja nae akisongea, pole pole (you see one by one changing accordingly, slowly slowly). Interview 3 Jane 13 February 2014. The Headteachers also promised scenarios to motivate the teachers. Most teachers did not have their children attending the schools they teach. The Headteachers provided scenarios as noted. "usually tell them" just put yourself in this parents shoes, that this is your daughter that is being neglected… but remember your daughter, wherever they are they are being taught by those teachers" (Interview 3 Jane 13 February 2014). With transport allowance well beyond their actual transport cost, the teachers felt motivated by the gesture. Finally the Headteachers encouraged the teachers to love and embrace their work.

Summary

The NEP trends over the eight years for the 15 school ranged between -0.002 and -33.93. Over the eight years the rate of change of the mean score was -5.29 with the mean averaging at 234.15 out of a possible maximum of 500. Only one school had a positive trend over the eight years. A comparison of pre and pre-ELMT brought out four schools that had an improving NEP trends.

The Headteachers leadership styles were included authoritarian, participative, and delegative. Participative style cut across all the Headteachers. The laissez faire styles did not appear for any of the Headteachers. Transformation leadership identified the Headteachers as strong in social and vision factors. The preferred leadership brought out all the Headteachers as being in leadership or tending towards leadership. The leadership matrix placed all the Headteachers in the team leadership category. Although they were in this category some were just entering the categories while the others were more developed in the category. The Headteachers displayed different strengths in human relationships. Strengths were in genuineness, self-exploration, empathy, correctness and immediacy. Mid-levels human relationships were confrontation and initiative. Self-disclosure, feelings and respect were weak areas expressed by the Headteachers.

According to the teachers, the Headteachers had changed on their leadership. There was an element of support, inclusion and empowerment of the teachers by the Headteachers. The Headteachers was working closely with the teachers involving them in both solving problems and school developmental plan. There were changes observed in the Headteacher governance some of which included resource management. The teachers expressed bias in the Headteachers and also needed more support in classroom observation and feedback.

The learning environment brought out a slightly above the median on the scale of excellence. The class-, teacher-, and gender responsive- excellence all scored above mid-point (Figure 9). The respective averages for the three aspects were 69.44%, 58.07% and 54.44% respectively. The cumulative average of 58% of the expected 100% on excellence was observed.

The type of teams in the schools indicated the type of leadership by the Headteachers. The teams in the school were at different stages based on the tasks and the length of interaction. Similarly the team leadership was mainly horizontal with only one Headteacher leadership lying between horizontal and vertical. The Headteachers expressed challenges in empowerment and collaboration in teams with motivation, modeling support and management featuring sparingly. The Headteachers used several approaches to overcome challenges in the teams. Some of the approaches were motivation, encouragement and priority setting.

The Headteachers identified networking with BOM, PTA and government as responding to quality assurance, management support and support and conflict management. The teachers had a different perspective on BOM and PTA. They knew their roles and felt that BOM and PTA did. The teachers were disappointed with BOM's and PTA's level of education. The teacher considered the government as supportive but decried on the numbers of teachers in the schools and the support they got from the government in terms of sponsorship.

The level of implementation was linked to the level of understanding the concepts. Two thirds of the implementation was in the topics of managing resources, leadership and pedagogical leadership equally implemented. The other third was action research, emerging issues, guidance and counseling, reflective practice and networking in that order in order of understanding and frequency of implementation. The understanding of the topics was between fair and good. The frequency of implementation was mainly occasionally and always at equal levels. The weighting of the topics resulted to 55% percentage level of understanding and 55% level of implementation. There percentages were similar cumulatively but there was not congruency on the responses between understanding (fair and good) and implementation (always and occasionally). Cumulatively there was an alignment between the levels of understanding and implementation.

The Headteachers perspectives on Broad and Newstrom's actions before, during and after the training fell in the categories of always, frequently and occasionally. Most of the actions were done always and an equal number of actions were done either frequently or occasionally. During the training the Headteachers were frequently doing most of the Broad and Newstrom's actions. A few actions were occasionally done due to the design of the training. The Headteachers categorized the Broad and Newstrom's action as always and frequently done after the training.

The Headteachers ranked Newstrom's barriers which were compared with Newstrom's ranking. The comparison showed mixed relationships. There was a flip on the ranking where Newstrom's great impact ranking were Headteacher's mild impact ranking. The least barriers had similar ranking. There was one outlier which was considered a great impact by Newstrom's but the Headteachers ranked it as the least barrier.

Newstrom's barriers were categorized to have impacts either as primary or secondary. Newstrom impacts varied based on the timeline of before, during and after EMLT. The Headteachers categorized the impact of the barriers and the Headteachers categorization was compared with Newstrom's categories. Before the training there were two barriers which were categorized as primary for both Headteachers and Newstrom's categorization. One barrier was flipped on impact. Newstrom's uncategorized barriers were seen as primary (2 barriers) and Secondary (4 barriers). During the training Newstrom's uncategorized barriers were categorized by Headteachers as primary impact (1 barrier) and secondary impact (2 barriers). 2 categorized barriers were similar to Headteachers and Newstrom's categories. 3 barriers alternated between primary and secondary impact for the Headteachers and Newstrom's categories. After the training Newstrom's uncategorized barriers were considered by the Headteachers as having secondary impact. 2 barriers had similar impact for both the Headteachers and Newstrom. 4 barriers flipped in categories as Headteachers found them as having secondary impact while Newstrom categorized them as having primary impact.

The Headteachers strongly agreed on all the statements given by Coates (2007). The statement referred to the organizational support which influenced performance improvement. The preferred school behavioral modes were in three categories. All the schools apart from one operated predominantly on a supportive mode which was leadership invested upon power. The school that was not predominant supportive was predominant custodial where paternalism was in practice. The other dominant mode was collegial mode which is a team concept that depends upon the management building partnership with the teacher.

The main barriers were teachers and resources which were inhibiting the transfer of ELMT skills. Other barriers of which emerged with lesser prominent but with equal distribution were culture/emerging issues, stakeholders (parents), teams, and policy. Teachers were the main stumbling block for the transfer in training skill in the school governance. The issues with teachers included attitude, change, commitment, delegation, economic, parents, resistance, resources, role modeling, and sensitization team work. Resources posed a barrier to Headteachers ELMT transfer of skills. All aspects of resources physical, time and financial posed barriers. The physical resources were those linked to the innovative approaches being introduced by the Headteachers. Culture of the school was a key barrier. Teachers were comfortable with the status quo and were not ready to take risks and try out new approaches.

Several themes came up with managers and stakeholders support taking the most prominence. Others aspects included appreciating change, fear (information provided before the training, networking and empowerment), participation during training, teamwork, managing resources and motivation. The school manager namely TSC and MoEST played key roles in overcoming the barriers in the transfer of ELMT skills to school governance. To overcome the barriers the Headteachers cited support from different sectors. Their main support was from the stakeholders. Others included mechanisms and amount of support, professional learning opportunities and action research. The Headteachers were coming up with innovative ways of governing schools after ELMT having gone through exposure to possibilities of change. Fear was an element that could be managed to overcome the barriers. The Headteachers cited that the fear could be overcome by the information of ELMT being provided in digital including level of encouragement and tasks before ELMT. Participating in the training was one thing the Headteachers cited as a way of overcoming the barriers, according to the Headteachers the practical and hands on experiences during the training gave them opportunity to understand concepts in a peer environment. The Headteachers realized the importance of forming teams among teachers, parents and students within the team's consultations and advice seeking was nurtured. Dialogue was encouraged in the teams and the team members freely expressed their views. Another aspect that enabled the Headteachers to overcome barriers during the ELMT skill transfer was the management of resources. This began by the resource mobilization through fund raising, donor sensitization and exploration of local, low cost, no cost resources. The Headteachers identified motivation as a basic need with multiple returns. They began the motivation by provision of basics like tea and lunch which allowed the teachers to stay in school and enhanced productivity.

Chapter 5: Conclusions and recommendations

This chapter provides creative thoughts and perspectives based on the findings of the study. The chapter offers the summary and recommendations for practical applications, way forward and further research. The chapter will share the implications of the level of ELMT skills transfer in schools, barriers identified and the approaches to overcoming the barriers.

Summary of the Results

This section covers the entire study with the problem statement, the studies' significance and summaries of literature review, methodology and findings.

Problem statement

To ensure that Headteachers are equipped with the knowledge, skills, and abilities to perform their duties effectively by attending in-service training such as ELMT. The Headteachers are strongly encouraged to take PLS by MoEST and TSC for reasons such as training, promotion and the need for new knowledge, skills and abilities.

The Kenya National Examination Council (KNEC) (2012) reports that, National Examination mean grade between 0-250 marks have been decreasing at a rate of -0.246 in the last five years. The discrepancy in the trends is contrary to the expected outcome after the Headteachers have attended ELMT. NEP at primary school has become the key aspect of measuring school performance. Educational leadership and its development are essential in improving school performance, hence raising educational standards (Wango, 2009). Current research shows that the leadership of a school is a critical factor in turning around low-achieving schools (Crew, 2007; Norguera & Wang, 2006). The leadership is enhanced by attending professional learning sessions. There are several factors which influence the transfer of training and they include the trainee, the school culture and the managers among others. These factors influence how the training skills are transferred to school governance. Complete transfer will influence school governance which may lead to an impact on the NEP trends. The complex nature of schools requires leaders to have the ability to be thoughtful and thorough, as well as courageous, humble, and emphatic in order to address these multifaceted challenges. On the other hand, NEP is high stakes, as it determines the ranking of schools both at district, county and national levels. It also determines the students' transition to secondary and measures the effectiveness of school governance. NEP trends among other factors are thus correlated to the effectiveness of school governance by the Headteachers. Meanwhile, being a Headteacher was based on either being an exemplary teacher, maturation in the profession, knowing someone in the administration, attending PLS or excelling in an extra-curricular event (Ministry of Education, 2008). Based on the identified basis of becoming a Headteacher, the only professional capacity building approach was through PLS; otherwise the position was attained without any education leadership and managerial training. Both the current status of NEP trends and the headship appointments prompted MoEST and TSC to advice the Headteachers to attend PLS such as ELMT. The reason for the advice was to empower the Headteachers, to govern their schools effectively and as a result improve on NEP. However the NEP trends were not indicative of the MoEST and TSC expectations. The dismissal NEP trends were still occurring even after the Headteachers had attended PLS such as ELMT. Evidently, some Headteachers had returned to pre-ELMT practice, having earned a certificate and/or a promotion, others have become effective school governors as a result of ELMT. The differences in effectiveness, have become a serious issue to the extent that the TSC has directed that school Headteachers' tenure in office to be pegged on the NEP trends and that any Headteacher who doesn't attend a PLS within two years risks losing the teaching license or be demoted.

The rush to attend PLS has been interpreted by MoEST as mainly for the sole purpose of acquiring papers rather than skills for competency (Ministry of Education, 2008). This was contrary to the assumptions by the MoEST and TSC that PLS were usually designed and implemented so as to empower the Headteachers with appropriate skills for effective governance of their schools (Ministry of Education, 2008). The Headteachers and the MoEST appeared to be conflicting on the purpose of PLS.

On the other hand, Headteachers had decried the quality of the PLS they were asked to attend (Gioko, 2011). Gioko (2013) acknowledges the design of the PLS as one element that influences the uptake and sustainability of the skills learnt. Moreover, Newstrom (1986) identified several factors known to affect the transfer of training. These included: individual learners, training programs, work environment, trainee's immediate manager/supervisor. Although the levels of transfer of the ELMT skills were not known yet, the information on whether this transfer was effective in schools with improving NEP trends was of crucial importance to all education stakeholders. This study aimed to explore how the Headteachers transferred the ELMT skills they were exposed to governance of their schools. It also sought to develop a deeper understanding of what exactly the Headteachers implemented. Furthermore, the study analyzed how business management skills could be infused in the transfer of ELMT skills. The outcomes will inform how to design future school leaders' preparation programmes for effective school governance.

Significance of the study

This study is the first formal study conducted in connection with ELM course, offered at the Aga Khan Academy Mombasa to Mombasa and Kwale county School Leaders. The results of this study will serve as a foundation to conduct more extensive studies with the project manager, facilitators, graduates and current course participants of ELM program. This study will contribute to educational research in the areas of course design, leadership training, school management and educational communities of practice for school support programmes.

There is need to understand the transfer of ELMT skills in school governance so as to understand on how to design ELMT and to track the return of investment. School leadership unlike many other organizations, is considered to be an essential service which requires school leaders to be on the cutting edge and equipped with the ability to implement best practices. On this premise, transfer of training is crucial in school governance and knowing how it happens successfully in the schools will identify ways of facilitating the transfer. The findings will have significant implications for the design and implementation of Headteachers' training programs and policies. One conclusion that emerges from a review of this research is that training is paramount to the effectiveness of training and education programs.

Benchmarking the ELMT skill transfer against competitors served as a catalyst for debate of what the stakeholders really value (Bowman & Schoenberg, 2008). Offering value in ELMT skill transfer will depend on the knowledge of the target course participants by understanding their needs and how they evaluate different product offering (Bowman & Schoenberg, 2008). The target groups were teachers in school, parents and the community. According to Hamels work, the Headteachers will need to re-conceive the existing models of school governance in a way that will create value and offer opportunities to the stakeholders (Bowman and Schonberg, 2008). The knowledge of the skills possessed and the projected stakeholders' demands will offer leverage during the ELMT skill transfer design. Bowman and Schoenberg (2008) demand the importance of understanding the criteria the stakeholder uses to evaluate the ELMT skill transfer. Furthermore, knowing the stakeholders' perception and experiences on ELMT skill transfer and cost will enhance competitive positioning (Bowman & Schoenberg). Bowman and Schonberg advice that systematic exploration of stakeholders' needs, perception and continuous listening to stakeholders could lead to the discovery of what is valued in the ELMT skill transfer and the services and what could be done to improve the perceived use value. Stakeholder's evaluation and feedback was undertaken as a strategic development from the demand side (Bowman & Schoenberg, 2008). Bowman and Schoenberg (2008) suggest that unconstructive buildup of stakeholder's perception of the ELMT skill transfer performance and the competitors will guide the competitive strategy of winning the ELMT sessions in the stakeholder's eyes –perceived use value and price.

The approaches will also bring opportunities of understanding how to infuse the knowledge learnt in BMC to ELMT to make it more effective and highly impacting. Meeting the objectives of the ELMT is very crucial. Substantial finance and time resources have been used by MoEST and other non-governmental institutions to plan and offer PLS. For example, the ELMT objectives are to improve education standards in respective schools. Hence, it must be important to understand the factors that influence the achievement of the objectives, as well as realize the return on investment (ROI). Headteachers have been seen as key in managing change in their schools for improvement. Hence, the research results informed the transfer of ELMT skills in school governance to facilitate increasing NEP trends. It also helped understand how the knowledge gained from the management course could be infused into the ELMT, to offer more effective knowledge, skills and values for school Headteachers. Insights informed ways of revising the ELMT, to ensure an improved success rate. With an opportunity to train over 300 Headteachers in the coastal counties, developing an effective model of training might attract MoEST to buy-in and take-up to over 32,000 Headteachers country wide (AKFC, 2011). Therefore, it's important to come up with ELMT which is effective and has high impact on school governance. The exploration brought insights on how timelines influences implementation practices. It also identified the aspects of training which have been sustained over time. Furthermore, the exploration brought forth any adaptation on skills offered. This information will be crucial in designing ELMT as well as exploring structures to support the implementation of ELMT skills. At the moment, MoEST through KEMI has initiated a training endeavor on educational leadership and management for all the Headteachers in primary schools. The findings of this research will be instrumental in influencing policy on ELMT. Currently, there are no studies that explore the transfer of ELMT skills in school governance. On this note, it is imperative that training institutions shared provide sufficient evidence that the training efforts are being fully utilized (Hunter-Johnson & Closson, 2011; Velada et al., 2007). Having concrete solutions in mind to handle potential barriers to change makes it more likely that leaders will translate their learning into action back at the workplace (Suinn, 1990). The findings of this study expanded the body of knowledge about barriers of training transfer for Headteachers. The study reinforced the importance of overcoming challenges, through innovative and reflective practices to implement the skills acquired in school governance.

The goal of this study was to help contribute to a body of practices and strategies for schools across the county. The insights gained from documenting and exploring the transfer of skills in school governance was instrumental in identifying how the Headteachers overcome the barriers. Opportunities were also explored on how to infuse the business management skills in school governance. The findings also served as testimonials and inspiration for aspiring Headteachers working in similar contexts.

Last and most importantly, this study served as evidence of the possibilities and as a promise to stakeholders that entrust their Headteachers to attend PLS. There are Headteachers who are willing to implement the skills learnt to school governance for the improvement of NEP trends but they need to be skilled on how to overcome the barriers they will face on re-entry in the schools.

Literature review

The review of literature focused on the transfer of skills after a period of training, barriers to transfer of skills, the ranking of the barriers, and the actions of the CP's and the impact of the barriers before, during and after the training and the business management skills applicable in managing or overcoming the barriers to the transfer of training.

The literature stipulates that there are factors that the Headteachers explored for them to decide what to implement from the dearth of information that they received in ELMT. It was also noted that the transfer of skills was a continuous process after the training. The time after training was seen as a factor with various researchers giving different percentages of what is applied and the failures and investment results. Several barriers have been identified as being the barriers for transfer of skills. The barriers have been ranked with the greatest referring the leadership theoretical views and the least referring to leadership philosophy endorsed by the organization. The barriers to training have different impact at different times, before, during and after the training. Several aspects have been given by research to explain how the impact of the barriers varies at different timelines. Dominant sources of the transfer of training barriers have been identified in the CP, trainer, manager and the organization. This brought to fore the exploration of the individual characteristics and organization factors and their role on the transfer of skills. Selected business management concepts have been reviewed as present to offer a possible solution to overcoming the barriers to transfer of skills. Hotspots have been identified as an approach that can be used to nurture the people supporting the transfer of skills. Focusing on the vital few has been presented as an aspect that can ensure that the focus is on the trivial many and the vital few in case of successes and converse in case of challenges to transfer of skills. Aspects of strategic planning have been explored indicating that the Headteachers could be empowered by the approach by offering a competitive advantage. The concepts of teams have established how they can be handled to enable the Headteacher succeed in the transfer of skills. The leadership styles have been found to be varying as the Headteachers transfer their skills, it has been seen that tasks and people will influence the type of leadership enabling the transfer of skills. The management skills have also been found to play a role where advanced strategic management will be instrumental. Management is resources including human resource. The review indicates that the Headteachers should take HR roles leading to strategic advantages. Performance tracking, value creation and value addition have been identified as playing a key role in strategic management. The management of resources could be enhanced through outsourcing services allowing the Headteachers to focus on their core business. The transfer of skills can be equated to a project, hence project and processes management have been identified to play a role in enabling the transfer of skills. EO has also been established to provide dimensions that will offer a platform to address the barriers. EO does not stand alone as it influences the configuration of teams hence shaping SC.

Technology advancement has offered opportunities which could be explored to address the barriers presented. Technology could facilitate information access and networking among other things, and could be used to improve organizational effectiveness. Stakeholder's engagement has been explored to bring to fore their level of participation, support and how they could play a key role to the success of the transfer of skills. FPE means the Headteachers have become financial managers as they handle the FPE money in schools. The integration of advanced accounting systems including EVA will place the Headteachers at an advantageous position of overcoming the barriers. The take up of performance management will see them embracing ABC, BSC and EVA as organization performance management tools. The complementarity of the frameworks will empower the Headteachers to overcome some of the barriers.

The aim was to identify the percentage of implemented skills to practice, the barriers faced and how they were overcome. The review of literature brought to fore, the business management aspects and how they could be used to enhance the transfer of ELMT skills to school governance. These aspects were reviewed in light of how the Headteachers could manage the barriers. The outcome on the level of implementation of the business management skills will inform the recommendations for effective ELMT skills transfer to school governance.

Methodology

The research design was a case study which entailed a qualitative approach with a concurrent triangulation strategy using qualitative data. Headteachers hold the primary role of taking up new knowledge and skills they are exposed to in ELMT. The implementations of the ELMT skills were explored through the objectives of the ELMT. The assumptions in the study were that the Headteachers gained their leadership skills through PLS they attended where ELMT was one of them. The exploration was done for two cohorts, one being 4 years after the training and another 3 years after the training. The Headteachers were profiled to collect data on their professional development over the years and their years of tenure as Headteachers were used. Trend analysis will bring out trends in different categories, such as increasing, static and decreasing NEP trends. Case study approach was deployed, where ELMT was a case in a bounded system that is, Headteachers in the coastal county of Kenya with NEP being the case descriptor. The outcome of the qualitative study was bound to reflect the reality on the ground. The qualitative approach allowed the shedding of light on the particular phenomenon (transfer of ELMT skills) in its natural setting (school governance). Qualitative research does not seek to establish generalizations that are universal and context free.

The total number of public primary schools in the coastal county was 115. The county was divided into four districts and 5 zones in each district. The sampling approach was based on purposive sampling to select cases which present increasing NEP trends, between pre- and post-ELMT. First and foremost, the participants were willing to participate in the research and were selected when they acknowledged understanding what the participants entailed. The teachers involved were in years 1, 3 and 6. These groups of teachers in one way or another experienced the school governance hence, their involvement enriched the data. Prior to conducting the primary study, a pilot study was conducted to provide reliability for the profiling, leadership (styles, preference, and networking), team (leadership and working together), barriers, organization impact and actions before, during and after training and open – ended interview protocol. The emergent, generalized statements from the findings were evaluated again through checks on the data.

Data collection involved drawing from multiple sources of information such as interviews, artifacts, documents (current/archival records) and observations (direct/participants). For the questionnaire and open-ended interviews, the meetings took place at an agreed location, which was conducive to open and candid communication. The Headteachers were interviewed and data was recorded and transcribed. Interviews were conducted on one-on-one basis and lasted 30 - 45 mins. Semi structured and open-ended interviews were used. Teachers were interviewed in a focus group and given the heavy demands on teachers; three teachers from lower middle and upper primary were interviewed in focus groups. After each interview session a summary was prepared. In addition to interviews, there were observations in several areas like classrooms, staffroom, departmental meetings, and interaction among respondents. This involved the documents which were related to school governance directly or indirectly. The instruments included but were not limited to leadership forms, interview protocol, observation protocol and artifacts analysis protocol. Throughout the research, the researcher maintained a reflective journal.

Unaeza and Gioko (2010) observe that familiarization with the context and the content of research enabled the researcher to have insightful experience in data collection and meaning making process. There were attempts to strengthen the credibility of the findings by further eliciting participant validation. Pseudonyms were adapted from official designations, and the corresponding abbreviated codes were used henceforth to indicate sources for quoted material. The data was organized with the major framework of levels of implementation, barriers and approaches of overcoming the barriers. Data analysis was time consuming and a complex process which included making sense of forms filled questionnaire responses, interview transcripts, observations, and artifacts analyzed. The emergent, generalized statements from the findings were evaluated again through thorough checks on the data. For the categories and patterns that seem so apparent, other plausible explanations and linkages were found for such situations where majority were in agreement over an issue, but some thought differently.

Findings

The NEP trends over the eight years for the 15 school ranged between -0.002 and -33.93. Over the eight years the rate of change of the mean score was -5.29 with the mean averaging at 234.15 out of a possible maximum of 500. Only one school had a positive trend over the eight years. A comparison of pre and post-ELMT brought out four schools that had an improving NEP trends.

The Headteachers leadership styles included authoritarian, participative, and delegative. Participative style cut across all the Headteachers. The Laissez faire styles did not appear for any of the Headteachers. Transformation leadership identified the Headteachers as strong in social and vision factors. The preferred leadership brought out all the Headteachers as being in leadership or tending towards leadership. The leadership matrix placed all the Headteachers in the team leadership category. Although they were in this category some were just entering the categories while the others were more developed in the category. The Headteachers displayed different strengths in human relationships. Strengths were in genuineness, self-exploration, empathy, correctness and immediacy. Mid-levels human relationships were confrontation and initiative. Self-disclosure, feelings and respect were weak areas expressed by the Headteachers.

According to the teachers, the Headteachers had changed on their leadership. There was an element of support, inclusion and empowerment of the teachers by the Headteachers. The Headteachers were working closely with the teachers involving them in both solving problems and school developmental plan. There were changes observed in the Headteacher governance some of which included resource management. The teachers expressed bias in the Headteachers and also needed more support in classroom observation and feedback.

The learning environment brought out an above average on the scale of excellence. The class-, teacher-, and gender responsive- excellence all scored above mid-point (Figure 9). The respective averages for the three aspects were 69.44%, 58.07% and 54.44% respectively. The cumulative average of 58% of the expected 100% on excellence was observed.

The type of teams in the schools indicated the type of leadership by the Headteachers. The teams in the school were at different stages based on the tasks and the length of interaction. Similarly the team leadership was mainly horizontal with only one Headteacher leadership lying between horizontal and vertical. The Headteacher expressed challenges in empowerment and collaboration in teams with motivation, modeling support and management featuring sparingly. The Headteacher used several approaches to overcome challenges in the teams. Some of the approaches were motivation, encouragement and priority setting.

The Headteachers identified networking with PTA/BOM and government as responding to quality assurance, management support and support and conflict management. The teachers had a different perspective on PTA/BOM. They knew their roles and felt that PTA/BOM did. The teachers were disappointed with PTA/BOM's level of education. The teacher considered the government as supportive but decried on the numbers of teachers in the schools and the support they got from the government in terms of sponsorship.

The level of implementation was linked to the level of understanding the concepts. Two thirds of the implementation was in the topics of managing resources, leadership and pedagogical leadership equally implemented. The other third was action research, emerging issues, guidance and counseling, reflective practice and networking in that order in order of understanding and frequency of implementation. The understanding of the topics was between fair and good. The frequency of implementation was mainly occasionally and always at equal levels. The weightings of the topics resulted to 55% percentage level of understanding and 55% level of implementation. There percentages were similar cumulatively but there was not congruency on the responses between understanding (fair and good) and implementation (always and occasionally). Cumulatively there was and alignment between the levels of understanding and implementation.

The Headteachers perspectives on Broad and Newstrom's actions before, during and after the training fell in the categories of always, frequently and occasionally. Most of the actions were done always and an equal number of actions were done either frequently or occasionally. During the training the Headteachers were frequently doing most of the Broad and Newstrom's actions. A few actions were occasionally done due to the design of the training. The Headteachers categorized the Broad and Newstrom's action as always and frequently done after the training.

The Headteachers ranked Newstrom's barriers which were compared with Newstrom's ranking. The comparison showed mixed relationships. There was a flip on the ranking where Newstrom's great impact ranking were Headteacher's mild impact ranking. The least barriers had similar ranking. There was one outliers which was considers great impact by Newstrom's by the Headteachers ranked it as the least barrier.

Newstrom's barriers where categorized to have impacts either as primary or secondary. Newstrom impacts varied based on the timeline of before, during and after EMLT. The Headteachers categorized the impact of the barriers and the Headteachers categorization was compared with Newstrom's categories. Before the training there were two barriers which were categorized as primary for both Headteachers and Newstrom's categorization. One barrier was flipped on impact. Newstrom's uncategorized barriers were seen as primary (2 barriers) and Secondary (4 barriers). During the training Newstrom's uncategorized barriers were categorized by Headteachers as primary impact (1 barrier) and secondary impact (2 barriers). 2 categorized barriers were similar to Headteachers and Newstrom's categories. 3 barriers alternated between primary and secondary impact for the Headteachers and Newstrom's categories. After the training Newstrom's uncategorized barriers were considered by the Headteachers as having secondary impact. 2 barriers had similar impact for both the Headteacher and Newstrom. 4 barriers flipped in categories as Headteachers found them as having secondary impact while Newstrom categorized them as having primary impact.

The Headteachers strongly agreed on all the statements given by Coates (2007). The statement refereed to the organizational support which influenced performance improvement. The preferred school behavioral modes were in three categories. All the schools apart from one operated predominantly on a supportive mode which was leadership invested upon power. The school that was not predominant supportive was predominant custodial where paternalism was in practice. The other dominant mode was collegial mode which is a team concept that depends upon the management building partnership with the teacher.

The main barriers were teachers and resources which were inhibiting the transfer of ELMT skills. Other barriers of which emerged with lesser prominent but with equal distribution were culture/emerging issues, stakeholders (parents), teams, and policy. Teachers were the main stumbling block for the transfer if training skill in the school governance. The issues with teachers included attitude, change, commitment, delegation, economic, parents, resistance, resources, role modeling, and sensitization team work. Resources posed a barrier to Headteachers ELMT transfer of skills. All aspects of resources physical, time and financial posed barriers. The physical resources were those linked to the innovative approaches being introduced by the Headteachers. Culture of the school was a key barrier. Some of the detrimental cultures were the drilling to kill, the Headteacher being the ultimate leader, lack or reading for students, the teachers the source of learning and the qualification of the teacher being enough with no room for further learning. This belief and practices are embedded in the teachers and the school making it a detrimental culture. Teachers were comfortable with the status quo and were not ready to take risks and try out new approaches.

Several themes come up with managers and stakeholder support taking the most prominence. Others aspects included appreciating change, fear (information provided before the training, networking and empowerment), participation during training, teamwork, managing resources and motivation. The school manager namely TSC and MoEST played key roles in overcoming the barriers in the transfer of ELMT skills to school governance. To overcome the barriers the Headteachers cited support from different sectors. Their main support was from the stakeholders. Others included mechanisms and amount of support, professional learning opportunities and action research. The Headteachers were coming up with innovative ways of governing schools after ELMT having gone through exposure to possibilities of change. Fear was an element that could be managed to overcome the barriers. The Headteachers cited that the fear could be overcome by the information of ELMT being provided in digital including level of encouragement and tasks before ELMT. Participating in the training was one thing the Headteachers cited as a way of overcoming the barriers, according to the Headteachers the practical and hands on experiences during the training gave them opportunity to understand concepts in a peer environment. The Headteachers realized the importance of forming teams among teachers, parents and students within the team's consultations and advice seeking was nurtured. Dialogue was encouraged in the teams and the team members freely expressed their views. Another aspect that enabled the Headteachers to overcome barriers during the ELMT skill transfer was the management of resources. This began by the resource mobilization through fund raising, donor sensitization and exploration of local, low cost, no cost resources. The Headteachers identified motivation as a basic need with multiple returns. They began the motivation by provision of basics like tea and lunch which allowed the teachers to stay in school and enhanced productivity.

Discussion of the Results
ELMT skills implemented

Leadership

The performance of the schools was generally declining and this could be one of the reasons that the MoEST and TSC raised alarm regarding the need for PLS and whether the training was effective. Despite general declining trends, there were a few schools that showed an improvement of the trends post ELM. 26% of the sampled schools showed improved post – ELM NEP trends. The fact that the sampling was representative clearly showed chances of only a quarter of the prepared Headteachers improving their NEP trends after post-ELMT. That indicated a need to dwell deeper and identify the level of implementation of the ELMT skills and the related aspects of barriers and how the barriers were handled.

The level of implementation of the ELMT skills took a broad approach and explored leadership teams and networking. It also took both a guided approach to understand the level of content understanding and examples of implementation. This was finalized by open ended questioning. The leadership styles were predominating participative and authoritative. The Headteachers had authority and they kept it close to themselves as delegation was either absent or scarce. It's clear that the Headteachers were still very authoritative welding power but not influencing their changes. The Headteachers were expected to be transformational leaders after ELMT. The transformational leadership by the Headteachers was well distributed with dominance in social and vision factors. As per the ELMT, the Headteachers were requested to have a fair distribution with least practices in transactional and laissez faire styles. The Headteachers did not have one leadership style. They displayed several types and mostly on tastes. According to Lewis, Welsh, Dehler and Green (2002) the Headteachers should be displaying different leadership styles as the transfer progresses. Robinson (2002) advocates for the Headteachers to develop positive relations skills and interrelationships. Jeffering, Michael and Shin (2003) suggest participative leadership which is associated with innovative success. As pedagogical leaders, the leadership of the Headteachers was demonstrated by how the classes were being delivered. The classroom, leader and gender responsiveness were scored above mid- point performance. The average of all aspects was 58%. Apparently the figure was similar to the levels of implementation which was 58%. Although there are no close links on the two. It seems like the Headteachers' implementation level influenced their outlook on their pedagogical leadership. The Headteachers had a balanced leadership factor.

The fact that the teachers noticed change was enough to indicate the impact of ELMT. The Headteachers seemed to have embraced the inclusion approach on decision making and effective resources management. The inclusion took a key consideration by the Headteachers using them to review school governance. The openness expressed by the Headteachers and the condition of expressing of their ideas on school governance was an indicator of the school culture offering up and embracing collective responsibility in school governance. Headteachers should be aware that the very basic assumptions of school culture itself may restrain the knowledge – transfer processes (Eskerod and Skiriver, 2007). The Headteachers should be aware of school culture as a phenomenon which has an impact on implementing new skills (Belassi et al., 2007). The Headteachers had been influenced by ELMT on inclusion and collective engagement. However issues of biasness and appraisal were areas the Headteachers needed to improve. The Headteachers might have been biased to buy clout of like-minded people but this should not be very obvious. Furthermore appraisal will inform the quality of teaching in the classroom. Hence as pedagogical teachers the Headteachers needed to make more observations in class and not just expect the mean score to improve.

Teams

The teams in the school according to Tuckmans model were in all categories of forming, norming, storming and performing. However the conflict level being of storming was rare. The teams in the school wanted to exist without going through the crucial step of storming. This was activated element in team formation. The performing level was based on tasks hence task driven or tenure in the school that is the longer the teachers stayed in the school the more they developed trust and moved their teams in the performing stage level.

The team leadership was mostly horizontal for all the Headteachers with only one being in between. Here the power dynamics did not work in team and the horizontal approach allowed more teams to thrive in the school. The characteristics of the teams were influenced by the governance which included the nature of leadership. However if there is need to understand the performance level of the teams with the fact that they missed the storming part and their task tenure based.

The teams under the Headteachers were not all smooth running as they faced challenges but they had elements of empowerment, collaboration, motivation, support and management. It was very clear that teams could not survive without challenges however it was the ability of the Headteachers to use the challenges as a learning opportunity. On the other hand the capitalizing on positive aspects of the team allowed the Headteachers to manage or overcome the challenges. The inclusion approach increased the participation. Hence, the Headteachers' delegative leadership approach allowed the teams to thrive. The success of the teams was based on the fact that the Headteachers were aware of what the challenges in the teams were, where they could be managed or eradicated. A broader analysis of the teams leads to a conclusion that teams will always have challenges however it's the handling of the challenges which will determine the success of the team. The other aspect is that positive aspects of the team outweighed the challenges hence the nurturing or provision of positive aspects in a team will facilitate the success of the team by overcoming the challenges. The Headteachers have embraced the teams unit in the ELMT course, as they found it inclusive, delegative and empowering. The fact that they realized teams enables them to govern their school and better influenced their uptake of team skills to practice.

Networking

Networking played a key role in school governance. ELMT had addressed the importance of networking to enhance school governance. Both the Headteachers and the teachers appreciated the governments' role especially on quality assurance and professional learning. However, even on this perspective the Headteachers and teachers felt that more needed to be done. This shows that the successful governance of the school will require more support by the government who were the managers of the school. The appreciation of the role of the government was an indicator of the extent the Headteachers had reached out and networked with the government as a crucial partner.

The downside of the networking was that BOM AND PTA who were seen by Headteachers as playing a minor role of conflict resolution. The BOM AND PTA were not involved enough in the school activities; some teachers did not even know them. Most of them were illiterate and did not participate or support teaching and learning. Although the ELMT prepared the Headteachers to involve the BOM AND PTA there were other challenges like illiteracy which the Headteachers could not address. The lack of support or involvement of BOM AND PTA in the school activities was an indicator that the Headteachers were struggling with this part of networking. The fact that the handicap was on school involvement and support could be an indicator of the declining NEP trends.

Levels of implementation

The level of implementation can be analyzed from leadership practices, teams in the schools and networking. A general analysis of these three aspects indicates that the Headteachers were in the processes of implementing the ELMT skills. There was a noticeable shift from the traditional school governance but the actual status was work in progress. However deeper analyses through both open ended and guided inquiry provided more details on the level of implementation. Most of the elements being implemented by the Headteachers were action research, emerging issues, guidance and counseling, reflective practice and networking. These are parts of the courses offered during the ELMT. An analysis to explore why they were implementing these courses only indicate that this were the courses where the Headteachers had a good or fair understanding of. These courses represented 55% of all the courses hence indicating that there was a relationship between what the Headteachers understood and what they implemented. The frequency of implementation of the identified topics was majority either occasionally or always. A weighing on implementation frequency indicated that the Headteachers implemented 55% of all the aspects they were exposed to. This is a sheer coincidence which indicated a relationship between the level of understanding and implementation. However it cannot be concluded as a correlation because individuals but commutatively the distribution between fair and good understanding was not similar to the distribution of frequency on occasionally and always. Baldwin and Ford (1998) observed the diminishing of knowledge with a lapse of time this support the 58% understanding of the concepts by the Headteachers. However, this percentage is held above Broad and Newstrom's (1992) and Bourke and Baldwin's (1999). Only 10% of the trainees were sampled hence Saks (2002) trainee's percentage of failure cannot be confirmed. This confirms the conclusion made from the general analysis of school governance. The levels of implementation are influenced by the level of understanding of the concepts. The Headteachers have tended to implement that they had a good or fair understanding on frequency of occasionally or always. The level of implementation can be confirmed to be slightly above half of the topics they were exposed to generally but with strengths in specific areas where they were not facing barriers or they were able to tame or manage the barriers.

Headteacher perspectives on barriers

The Headteachers perspectives were analyzed based on three aspects

- Newstrom's actions pre, during and post training.
- Organizational structures and behavioral models.
- Newstrom's barriers' ranking.
- Impact of Newstrom's Barriers Pre, during and Post training.

Headteachers perspectives on Newstrom's actions pre, during and post training

According to Newstrom (1986), there were actions by the course participants before, during and after the training which could influence the transfer of ELMT skills to practice. Newstrom had identified several actions which could be categorized in terms of frequency at different stages or of before training, during training and after training. The review of what was being implemented from ELMT triggered the exploration of what might have influenced the implementation levels. The frequency of the actions before training was evenly distributed between always, frequently and occasionally. The Headteachers responded to

Newstroms' action they were doing before training in the categories of always, frequently and occasionally. The Headteachers always did the activities before the training which addressed their preparedness for the course. The actions which were always preferred by the Headteachers were labeled as preparedness. They indicated on how ready the Headteachers were to undertake the course and what measures they had put in place to ensure they benefited fully from the course. The level of preparedness also included the understanding of the individual's performance gap and expectation before attending the course. For this group of the Headteachers' preparedness was crucial before attending ELMT. The level of preparedness explored the Headteachers' performance gap and attending the course because they needed it. There were aspects of ensuring what they were going to learn shunning negative feedback and managing possible distractions. The response indicates what was important to the Headteachers such as their need, what is being offered and how they will go through it comfortably. Therefore the core aspect of preparedness is linking the need to ELMT objective and the comfort of attending the ELMT.

The frequently done activities before the training, the Headteachers' ELMT included self and others. The Headteachers were self-focused on goal setting and being open-minded during the pre -ELMT activities. Others included delegation of duties and sharing of programs and expectations to the manager. Although their activities were done, the fact that these activities were done frequently rather than always could be an indication of the irregular attendance of the sessions. At times the Headteachers could ask for permission to attend to something in the office. The sharing of the program was also a frequent activity rather than always since the letters of selection went through the managers so the managers was aware of the program and its expectations. Good setting and open-mindedness were aspects which will influence their active participation in ELMT activities. The fact that this was not always will explain why for some instances the Headteachers will feel challenged to embrace ideas conflicting their current practice. Although the always responses represented the preparedness, the pre- ELMT activity which was done frequently meant that the level of preparedness was affected as the Headteachers did not do the pre-ELMT activities. The Headteachers got prepared to attend ELMT but limited to other factors other than pre ELMT activity. In their mind ELMT began when they attended the sessions. The frequently done activities impacted the transfer to some extent but they will be more effective if they were done always.

The activities which were occasionally done before the training catered for learning and participation. The Headteachers occasionally explored learning options or researched other related materials. The Headteachers were coming to the training without preparing to learn before the ELMT training. The Headteachers did not participate in the ELMT preparations such as gathering materials, developing questions, identifying case studies before the beginning of ELMT. This was the design of the curriculum which was prepared independently. The actions done occasionally indicated that the Headteachers were only concerned on ELMT when it began. The knowledge of the location, time and dress code did not have importance as the Headteachers were training at a location they already knew and also they had standards on the code of conduct.

The analysis of the actions before the training influenced the readiness of the Headteachers in attending the ELMT. Although most of the actions identified by Newstrom were done always, the actions done frequently and occasionally influenced the level of preparedness as well as indicated how motivated the Headteachers were. It can be concluded that the Headteachers were partially ready for ELMT based on the action they did before ELMT. But this cannot only be pointed to the Headteachers but also to the organization of the ELMT programs. Some of the activities could be initiated or triggered by the ELMT organizers. The transfer of skills in training is influenced by the activities before the training. However, these activities are the responsibility of the participants attending the training and the organization of the training. Both of them have a role in ensuring all the activities before the training are done always to facilitate the transfer of training skills to practice.

During the training, the frequency of Newstrom's identified actions fell into two categories of frequently and occasionally. Actions done always were lacking during the ELMT. Newstrom identified actions to be done during ELMT to facilitate transfer of skills. The Headteachers' responses categorized frequency as the actions predominantly frequent with some actions falling within occasionally. Most of the actions identified as frequently done had a linkage with the course design and the personal commitment of learners. The course design and the facilitator will take a key role in formulating the frequently done actions. The fact that there were no responses in the always category was reflection on both the ELMT design and the Headteachers. The occasional actions such as understanding could be reflected from the level of the Headteachers' responses on the level of understanding concepts. Making notes was not very necessary as the Headteachers were provided with handouts. However paying close attention and linking to buddies was something which should have appeared in always category. For this case it could be a parameter that influenced the extent of transferring the skills to practice. The actions during the ELMT were dependent on the course designs and the Headteachers themselves. It will be important for the course design to be aware of the required actions and create an environment where they can be enacted. It will also be important for the facilitators to implore on the participants and ensure they act the roles they are supposed to do. The extent of ELMT skills implemented after the training correlates to the responses on the action of the Headteachers during ELMT.

The post-ELMT actions were categorized better compared to the actions during ELMT. The actions fell in the category of always and frequently. The always actions belonged to course structure, support structure and individual disposition. The course structure had a practicum session and also required deliverables. This allowed the Headteachers to be able to turn principles into a project, develop short/ long term projects and develop job aids. Furthermore, the facilitation of professional learning network allowed the Headteachers to develop relationship, influence those involved and share learning principles, maintain contact with new networks and present findings to peers. The support structure from MoEST and TSC allowed the Headteachers to seek their support in implementing change of strategies as well as participate in the refresher courses. Individual disposition influenced provision of honest feedback to trainers as well as looking for behavior change.

The frequency done post ELMT action also focused on the support structures. This included the practicum sessions which allowed the Headteachers to practice self-management and practice continuously. The involvement of TSC and MoEST allowed the Headteachers to discuss performance objective and action plans with the Headteachers. Furthermore, the involvement of the quality assurance department of MoEST enabled the Headteachers to review content and learned skills. The structure required the writing of a reflection on what they had learned as well as follow- up through the professional learning network. Frequently, post ELMT actions were mainly influenced by course design and support structure. Although it was expected for all actions to fall within the always category, there were short falls which involved all the stakeholders namely trainers, manager and individuals. This confirms Newstrom's identified barriers of the three stakeholders as part of those that influence the transfer of training. Post-ELMT actions will be guided by the course structure, support structures and individual dispositions. Hence all the stakeholders need to understand the post-ELMT actions and facilitate them.

Headteachers' perspectives on organizational structures and behaviors models.

The organizational support will support or hinder the transfer of ELMT skills. The Headteachers agreed strongly on all the statement offered by Coates (2007). The organizational support was mainly from MoEST and TSC who are the managers of the Headteachers. These managers provided support in facilities, accountability on the Headteachers, modeling new practices, exploring Headteachers' expectations being involved on the

Headteacher's progress providing structures for progression and designing policies that will facilitate the implementation of the new approaches. A department of MoEST, QASO also played a key role in the organizational support. QASO support include performance goal setting and review as well as provision of incentives to motivate the Headteachers to implement new ideas. QASO and the course facilitators also did periodic impact studies which offered Headteachers' feedback and identified areas of potential improvements. Other organizational structures included PLN, KEPSHA, job description and course design. PLN and KEPSHA allowed the Headteachers to share their learning. The Headteachers' job description required them to use the skills and concepts they learnt at ELMT. The course design offered assignments and tasks that allowed the Headteachers to apply the knowledge learnt,

This analysis brings out the managers as the key facilitators of organizational support. Hence as MoEST and TSC demand for the Headteachers to attend PLS they should be aware of their key responsibility and its potential impact on the transfer of ELMT skills. The realization of their responsibility as not only sending teachers for ELMT but providing support might remove the blame game where Headteachers have been accused of not implementing what they have learnt. The success of transfer of ELMT skills has additional aspect of organizational support above managers, trainers and individuals.

Organizational culture has an impact on the level of transfer of ELMT skills. Rouiller and Goldstein (1995) support the Headteachers identification of culture as a barrier. According to Rouiller and Goldstein, organization factor guide the individual and ELMT transfer of skills transfer and contribute to organizational climate which could either support or inhibit the transfer. Kazlwoski and Salas (1997) observe that the organizational culture should be considered as interdependence between Headteachers, teams and the organization. Hence the consideration of culture should also be linked to the Headteachers and teams in the school. The Headteachers' preference on the organizational behavior steered off the experiences of never and always and was in the mainly occasionally and frequently. The tenure of the teachers in the school was permanent according to TSC and did not depend on NEP. Moreover the teachers were always required to put more than minimum effort in trying to improve the NEP.

The behaviors preferred occasionally by the Headteachers revolved around job security, commitment and leadership. The students in these categories were occasionally preferred because they were not favorable to an enriched learning environment. The Headteachers preferred more performance based jobs, inclusion and collaboration. This was confirmed by the frequently preferred behavior. These behaviors were inclusion, commitment and collaboration. The organizational behavior preferred by the Headteachers is where all teachers were active, involved and were committed to the performance of the school. Elements of teams and effort are key organizational behaviors preferred by the Headteachers. The behaviors for transfer ELMT skills were any behaviors on the contrary to the preferred behaviors. Although the schools had a tendency for a preferred behavior mode they were actually on transition mode apart from the some schools that did not fall among the others. The schools were on transition and had no predominant behavioral mode but some detrimental cultural practices were still etched in the practices.

Headteachers' perspectives on Newstrom's barriers' ranking

The understanding of these barriers was explored on how the Headteachers ranked barriers identified by Newstrom's (1986), perspective on the impact of the barriers before, during and after the training and their perceived barriers.

The ranking of the barriers by the Headteachers differed slightly with the Newstrom's ranking of the barriers. The barriers that focused on the trainer and training had a correlation in the ranking. They were considered to have least impact on the ELMT skill transfer. The Headteachers could develop a positive perception on the agency offering the training because the agency had a reputation. The swoop of the mild and great impact barriers was surprising. Newstrom's mild impact barriers were on the training and they focused on the perception on the training program, contact and comfort. Apart from relevancy of the contact, the other two aspects of impracticability of the training program and the problem of discomfort with change were considered as high impact by the Headteachers.

The Headteachers had preference on programs that respond to their needs and offers practical solutions to their problems. The Headteachers were also required to embrace or implement changes. This trend indicated the core aspects according to the Headteachers. The others indicated the impact of peers in the work place. Newstrom (1986) had ranked peer pressure as the least barrier but the Headteachers consider it the high implementing barrier. This indicates that the Headteachers considered their teachers as the main obstacle in transferring ELMT skills to practice. This was confirmed when the Headteacher responded to open ended questions.

Therefore Newstrom's (1986) ranking can be influenced by the Headteachers' preferences and their perspective on the barriers. The ranking cannot be generalized or considered for the impact of barriers on ELMT skills transfer to practice.

Perspectives on impact of barriers pre, during and post ELMT

The difference in ranking prompted further explorations of the Headteachers' perspective on the barrier. In this analysis the barrier were considered before, during, and after ELMT and whether at each of the stages they were either primary or secondary time impact. On the primary and secondary impact at different training times brought out different results compared to Newstrom (1986). The other (peer pressure) was swooped in the impact ranking; this was expected as it was on one another. Organizing culture and trainee discomfort were aligned for both the Headteachers and Newstrom. Newstrom's uncategorized aspects were considered primary impact by the Headteachers. To the Headteachers lack of empowerment and interference were prime barriers. This shows that the Headteachers were more concerned with support from managers and the environment which they were working in. Newstrom's least ranked and uncategorized barriers were in consent with the delivery inspiration, context and progress. The Headteachers could have considered these as secondary time impact due to the fact that the agency offering ELMT had a reputation. It is not clear why Newstrom left aspects uncategorized within the primary and secondary time impact.

Newstrom's barriers during the training were almost all categorized. The uncategorized aspects were categorized as primary and secondary by the Headteachers. Similarities were on comfort perception. The other barriers addressed the impact categories. During the training the similarity between the Newstrom's category and the Headteachers' was in only two barriers out of the nine identified barriers. After the training all the uncategorized barriers (perceptions) observed by the Headteachers to have a secondary time impact. There was alignment in two barriers, culture and peers which were different within the similarity on the impacts during the training. There was a flip in the categorization of inspiration, comfort, environment and reinforcement. The perspective on the impact of the barriers had a mixed outcome when compared to Newstroms' impacts. First the Headteachers ranked all barriers all the time there were six out of 27 ranking aspects were in agreement with Newstrom's ranking. Perspective on the impact of the barriers was contextual. The perspective on the impact will depend on the perspective of how the Headteacher weighs the barrier depending on their circumstances.

Headteachers' identified barriers and their relation to Newstrom's barriers

The analysis of the barriers revolved around ranking Newstrom's barriers, identifying the impact of different stages of the training, responding to Coates (2007) organizational support statement and categorizing the frequency of preferred organizational behaviors. These aspects were theoretical based and explored the Headteachers' experiences in light of the theories. Further exploration was Headteacher's identification of barriers without guidance.

The Headteachers identified six barriers to transfer of ELMT transfer of skills, the barriers were teachers, resources, policy, culture, support and students. The policy was inhibiting as there was unclear formulation on the nature of support the Headteachers were supposed to receive. Burke and Baldwin (1999b) demand that policy on support will influence transfer. Schools should have policies that safeguard the availability of finite resources for the future generations (Narveson, 2003). The school policies should look at these aspects to have an accommodating working environment beneficial to the school. There should be clear policies which guide the school to realize their goals without harm while being aligned to government policies. Crommal and Kolb have revealed that the four environmental factors of organization, supervision, peer and participation have a significant positive correlation with transfer. Three of these factors were also identified by Newstrom (1986). The Headteachers' barriers were in congruence to research findings.

The Headteachers found teachers and resources as the main barriers to ELMT skills transfer. The findings correspond to the Headteachers ranking peer pressure as the highest ranking Newstrom (1986) barriers to transfer of training. The barriers in teachers included attitude, change, commitment, delegation, economies, parent resistance, resources, role modeling, sensitization and team work. The resource barriers were both physical and time. Teachers formed the main barrier to transfer of training. There is need to understand as to why the teachers could be a stumbling block to the Headteachers whom they are supposed to work well with. Teachers and Headteachers have a voluntary engagement; teachers generally prefer more stable employment relationships, though they might be earning what they think they do not deserve as a matter of justice (Freeman & Rogers, 1999). Nerveson (2003) justifies the continued employment in a voluntary relationship as a matter of choice. Nerveson (2003) links employment engagement as a teacher selling service at a price that is being offered by the employer. The linkage is a mismatch between the preferences of Headteachers and teachers with regard to the employment relationship (Van Buren & Greenwood, 2008). In reality Headteachers had a notion that they were helping the teachers, while the teachers felt that they were helping the Headteachers. Such notions encourage unethical acts which erode the relationships between teachers and Headteachers. The relationship between the Headteacher and teachers need to be collegial with interdependence flavor nurturing support to among them

The barriers identified by the Headteachers did not fall in the trainee perceptions which Quinones (1995) includes that the trainee's perception raised the probability of bringing back the ELMT skills to the work place. The top three barriers ranked by Newstrom (1986) identified by the Headteachers included culture, policy, lack of reinforcement (support) and resources. Quinone, Ford, Sego and Smith (1995) classifies these barriers as demoralizing the Headteachers and making them find it harder to demonstrate their new skills hence not sustaining a behavior change desired. Ironically this identified barriers ranked as mild compared to Newstrom's ranking and they were considered to be second mostly likely to be a barrier after the training. Newstrom had considered the most likely barriers after ELMT. Teachers were the most predominant barrier in the transfer of ELMT skills. According to Newstrom (1986), peers were ranked the least barrier but the Headteachers ranked them as the greatest barrier which confirmed their identification of teachers as the main barrier. Apparently, Newstrom had also ranked peers (teachers) as the most likely barrier after training which concurred with the

Headteachers' rating of barriers after the ELMT training. The Headteachers have been consistent on the peers as the barriers. This is reaffirmed in the ranking and the likelihood. However, it contributes to the Newstrom's ranking which found peers as the least barrier. Apparently, Newstrom did not identify the clients as the barriers whereas in this case the Headteachers identified the students as the barriers. The Headteachers felt that the economic status of the students and the truancy did not allow them to implement the ELMT skills. Although this was considered as a separate barrier it can fall into the barrier of interference from immediate environment.

The identification of the barriers by the Headteachers confirms the greatest barriers identified by Newstrom. However, they did not identify any of the least barriers of Newstrom. The lowest ranking of the Newstrom's barrier was seen as the greatest barriers of all barriers. The Headteachers identified peer support as one of the major barriers; this is similar to the observation by (Facteau, Dobbins, Russel, Ladd, & Kudisch, 1995). Tracy, Tannenbaum and Kavanagh (1995) and Chin (2011) found that workplace, social and peer support for training can also influence transfer of training hence efforts should be made to ensure peer support is enhanced. Gratton (2007) advices that the transfer will be enhanced by the practices where she identifies collective reward, peer working and social support responsibly among the six practices. Quinone et al (1995) emphasized as perceived peer support at school which they claim has shown to predict the amount of perceived opportunities to use knowledge, skills and attitude following training. It is therefore imported to explore way in which teachers are treated equally and is nurturing of peer support through different approaches.

Headteachers management of barriers and recommended infusion of business management theories

The schools were experiencing changes with the return of Headteachers who had been exposed to multiple innovations on school governance. One approach the Headteachers used was appreciating the change they were going through. Newstrom (2008) has identified the resistance to change and the efforts required as a barrier to ELMT transfer of skills. Chin advocates for Headteachers to have support and accountability for change. This will help the Headteachers as they initiate or experience change. The Headteachers had groups of teachers demonstrating resistance to change; this was latent energy according to Gratton. Gratton advises the Headteachers not to give up but rather explore ignition such as igniting questions, igniting task or igniting vision. The Headteachers should not give in to teachers resisting the change. The exhibition of latent energy can be overcome with the three forms of ignition (Gratton, 2007). Furthermore the Headteachers should do force field analysis to establish the forces against or fore (Nugent, 2002). Harris and Cole (2007) cautions on the challenges to modify behavior of the resisting teachers will be futile unless the teachers are aware of benefits of change and what is required to embrace the change. The Headteachers accepted alternative ways they were exposed to during ELMT and the possibility of being applied in the schools. The alternatives were presented through awareness, acceptance and embracing of the ideas by the individuals. The appreciation was then extended to the many teachers that the Headteachers were working with in their schools. The Headteachers had to try and influence the teachers to embrace new approaches. Although the Headteachers expressed general views of influencing the teachers, there were several approaches they could have embraced from the business management concepts. One of the approaches is focusing on vital few. With the introduction of new ideas there will be few people who will embrace the ideas but they will be doing most of the implementation of the innovative ideas. The Headteachers will need to identify vital few of the whole who will be the champions of the new ideas as they were implementing 80% of the new ideas being tried out. There will be identification, motivation and provision of support to ensure that the teachers implemented the new ideas. Lammers and

Tsretko (2008) support the identified vital few that will mitigate the barriers. However Reh (2005) warns that it's not only the application of the rule that should be the focus but wisdom needs to be included. The Headteachers will need to balance the implementation of focusing on vital few to avoid blind spots among the trivial many and vital few.

Another business management concept will be the identification of Gratton's (2007) hotspots. As the change is being embraced the Headteachers should be able to identify the group of teachers who are jellying well and collaborating to implement the new ideas. This group should be supported through igniting-tasks and -visions to propagate the implementation the new ideas. The Headteachers should also be aware of the cold-freeze and work around it. The embracing of change will require the Headteachers to both focus on the vital few and implement Gratton's hotspots among others to influence the teachers. The Headteachers should be able to identify the three aspects that influence hotspots that is cooperative mind set, identifying the boundary spanner and sharing the igniting purposes (Gratton, 2007). This will allow Headteachers to reach out to the few who have taken up the new ideas and push them further. Gratton guides Headteachers to create cooperative environment which will then influence the implementation levels and the quality of interactions in schools.

The experiences during ELMT exposed the Headteachers to multiple approaches and innovations in school governance. During ELMT some Headteachers struggled to understand the new concepts they were exposed to. This explains the levels of implementation which has a correlation between what they understood or had grasped and what they implemented post ELMT. There was fear among the Headteachers as they felt overwhelmed by the multiple ideas and approaches they were exposed to. This links to the level of preparedness as the Headteachers attended ELMT. There is need to provide information about ELMT, level of commitment and assignments before the Headteachers are engaged in the training (Newstrom 2008). The Headteachers preparing to attend ELMT must be ready to learn hence a lot of preparedness should be done before the ELMT. The actions of the Headteachers before the ELMT indicate the level of preparedness. Colquitt, Lupine and Noe (2000) indicated the influence of pre- training self-efficacy on the significance of training. The Headteachers were in a way ready to learn as Hanna and Lester (2009) sees this as developmental readiness which will influence motivation and make meaning of the knowledge into one's long term memory structure. Argyns (1995) and Senge (1990) acknowledge the readiness as a shift in mind which will influence the Headteachers to take action after acquiring the new knowledge. The preparedness should include not just awareness but activities that will be insightful and develop in the Headteachers a purpose to learn and an understanding of what it will require to learn. The Headteachers took to networking with peers as one way of overcoming fear and learning from each other. Chin (2011) has advocated for peer support or networking as elements that could support change processes. According to Chin's (2011) description the Headteachers should explore structures for obtaining feedback and guidance such as coaching, mentoring and shadowing or observing successful cases of transfer of skills to be enhanced to develop a motivation of transferring ELMT skills. The element of networking can be enriched through the team's approach. The MoEST cluster structure which is geographical grouping of schools could be used to have cluster teams working together during and after the training. Working together and sharing ELMT skills transfer experiences will offer opportunities to transcend the barriers. To enhance the opportunities an inter-cluster engagement will facilitate further learning within and across clusters. The business management aspect of teams as opposed to working groups will provide a guidance and experience to overcome fears of ELMT skills transfer (Anne, 1993). Newstrom identified teams as an aspect during and after training action. The Headteachers were also in agreement to Newstrom's statements that they had to always maintain contact with in networks and present findings to peers.

The Headteachers felt supported by the managers (TSC and MoEST). They felt that being requested to attend the session by the managers was motivating. The involvement of the managers in their selection and sharing of content allowed the managers to know who was attending and what they were learning. According to the Headteachers' preferred organizational behavior, the Headteachers responded "frequently" to Coates (2007) statement of "Both managers and teachers want to create better job performance and managers display of real relationship traits that are respected by the Headteachers." p. 10. The inclusion of the TSC and MoEST to facilitate some of the sessions such as performance management (TSC) and financial Management (MoEST) presented a collaborative approach of delivering ELMT. This encouraged the Headteachers as they saw the managers' involvement and it also inspired a responsibility as the same managers will be involved in quality assurance and standards monitoring. This concurs with Coates (2007) strongly agreed statements on performance review and incentives (Table 17).

Table 17 Coates (2007) Statements on efforts to Improve

My performance goals and objectives require me to use the skills and concepts I learned in the training.

My performance review evaluates how well I'm using the skills and concepts I learned in the training.

The rewards and incentives available to me to motivate me to use the skills and concepts I learned in the training.

Note From *"Enhance the training of training: Tips, Tools and Intelligence for Trainers", By D. E* Coates, 2007. *0710.* (J. Brusino, Ed.) USA: ASTD. Pg 10.

The Headteachers felt fully supported by their managers as the mangers also offered supplementary courses through KEMI to support what they had learnt. This support concurs with Coates statements which were strongly agreed by the Headteachers. The approach also concurs with Newstrom's observation which indicated that managers play a key role in the transfer of ELMT skills to school governance. Baldwin and Ford (1998) identified work environment through supervisor support for learning and other application to be important elements for transfer of ELMT skills.

The Headteachers had cited fear as a barrier that they had to overcome and they explored several aspects to develop confidence and overcome fear apart from networking. The Headteachers acknowledged that participation during the training was crucial in overcoming the barriers of fear, building confidence and deepening understanding of the concepts. This confirms two aspects, their lack of always response on participation during the ELMT and Newstrom's identification of participation as a key action during ELMT to facilitate transfer. The Headteachers identified participation as a frequently done action and not always. Due to the frequency of active participation during ELMT the Headteachers came out with elements of fear which they had to overcome through networking after ELMT. It can be concluded that attendance to ELMT is not adequate and there is need to always participate actively and be engaged with the concepts relating them to work experiences (Newstrom, 2008). The participation will build confidence giving a leeway during the transfer of ELMT skills, ameliorating fears and increasing the possibilities of learning through networking.

Stakeholder's role was crucial on the ELMT transfer of skills to school governance. The key stakeholders were parents, students and the politicians who facilitated the transfer of ELMT skills. The stakeholders were instrumental in providing resources, systemic strengthening and incentives to the Headteachers and teachers in the schools. The involvement of stakeholders widened the number of people involved facilitating networking which was also a key element in overcoming the barriers. Teachers have long been recognized as school's stakeholders (Van Buren, 2003). Moreover teachers can be identified as moral claimant stakeholders to whom the school has morally obligatory perfect duties (Kaler, 2003). The level of involvement and commitment in teachers' practices had effects on Headteachers and teachers (Park, Appelbaum, & Kruse, 2010). Relationships with teachers should be explored in consideration with the potential of parents, Headteachers and teachers. The stakeholders include the community in which the school is situated since a school exists within a society as a third party (Nerveson, 2003). Engagement with the school community should not cause harm or deception to the teachers involved. The engagement of the school community should be based on mutual benefit for those involved and not be based on nepotism, tribalism or exploitation (Narveson, 2003).

The establishment of teams and facilitation of team's members and across teams was a unique way the Headteachers used to overcome some barriers. The Headteachers first reduced the number of people they were to deal with through the teams approach. The Headteachers also empowered the teams by allowing them to engage among themselves and across teams. There were different teams in every school. From the responses on teams and team leadership most teams in the schools were still on storming stage or stayed on the forming stage. The teams rarely progressed to norming and performing staged. The status of the team impacted on the level of ELMT skill transfer. Barczack, MeDenough and Athanassiou (2006) recommend open communication for the team members to be on the same page. According to Jungalwalla (2000), the Headteachers should implement strategies of understanding communication styles, paraphrasing to enhance active listening and finishing conversations with a question. Such an approach will enable the Headteachers to share their ideas ensuring all teachers understand. The Headteachers should facilitate the development of social capital in the team internal network through bonding time, sharing information, encouraging collaboration, identifying mutual relationships for maintaining commitment and motivation (Barczak, MeDonough & Athanassiou, 2006).

The effectiveness of the teams will be determined by the type of teams. The Headteachers should be aware that cross functional teams are beneficial in supportive organizational structures and practices (Anne, 1993). Such teams do not work well when teachers feel stressed, neglected by the school and unsure of the rewards they will receive (Hong, Hahn & Doll, 2004). According to Pons (2008) the Headteachers should try to develop cross functional team skills and experiences. The compositions of teams in urban settings are culturally, ethnically and functionally diverse (Grisham, 2010). Hence the Headteachers will need to recognize the quality of the mixed size and access the team's characteristics, marshal appropriate managerial skills and personal attributes to manage team diversity right from the onset. This is a similar approach to competencies as the knowledge of the team characteristics will allow the Headteachers to allocate tasks strategically. Pons (2005) recommends the Headteacher's role in managing the teams to include providing training and motivation, sorting out conflicts, appraising staff performance and helping in decision making. Gobedi, Koening and Bechinger (1998) advice that the Headteachers should be aware that small doses of conflicts proved to be beneficial. The Headteachers should be cognizant to the attributes to improvement which include sharing goals, responsibility for success, collegiality, continuous improvement, lifelong learning, risk taking, support, mutual respect, openness, celebration and humor (Stoll and Fink, 1996). Headteachers must ensure that the human capital of the team members is involved in the evaluation of member's social capital, during the process of team norming, forming, storming and performing (Stam & Elfring, 2008). Pidd (2001) identifies the influence of the support from the teams in the school. The support panels or year level leaders could provide support in the organizational structures that had policies and procedures advocating for that. According to Jorgensen and Emmitt (2009) the Headteachers should be aware of the importance to stimulate team learning and the exchange of knowledge at all levels of ELMT skill transfer and at all relevant levels of the departments involved.

The Headteachers were working in no-, low-resourced schools environment. Although resource was an issue, sourcing and managing was a related challenge. Schools were provided with some money for teaching resources which is managed by School Instruction Material Selection Committee (SIMSC). The Headteachers on the other hand did not have skills for procurement. What the Headteachers did was to maximize the use of minimum resources through scheduling. The Headteachers will be more empowered if they had embraced the outsourcing concept. The Headteachers had undergone a unit on managing resources which was part of ELMT. However, schools will not have the expertise to do all the services they will need to embrace outsourcing. The global changes demand effectiveness in management, which calls for a dedicated focus to strategic issues. Among the observed trends is management engaging expertise from profit seeking specialists who enjoy enormous economies of scale. For example, printing of termly examination or monthly tests a photocopy company can supply photocopies and manage them in a school instead of the school buying their own. Other areas of outsourcing will be text-books, IT and other teaching resources. Glassman (2000) argues that the opportunities are attributed to either the outsourced firm specializing or having a probability of innovation or more time allocated to key issues, because the vendor is running other issues. According to Glassman (2000) allocating specific roles to specialists and leaving the Headteachers with crucial roles are bound to impact on the effectiveness of the ELMT skill transfer.

ELMT equipped Headteachers with tools they could use in school governance, however the tools were either understated or unused (Drucker, 1995). Headteachers should be able to access information that allows them to make informed judgment. The diagnostics tools include foundation-, productivity-, competence- information and information about the allocation of scarce resources (Drucker, 1995). Drucker observes that the progression in advancement has outpaced the human rate of adoption. According to Drucker, there are many systems the Headteachers could use to govern schools such as traditional and activity costing. He outlines traditional as focusing on task only, while activity is all inclusive. The inclusiveness of the later approach provides cost information and yields control. The knowledge of such information will enable Headteachers to make decisions on which type of costing to use to realize effectiveness. Knowing about cost alone will not be successful as the knowledge of the entire financial chain will enable the management of costs and minimization of yield (Drucker, 1995). Costing in isolation will not yield much and needs to be integrated in the entire economic chain to increase cost advantage.

Managing resources include the teacher (HR) as a barrier. Murray (2008) observes that work trends are becoming unpredictable, varied and dynamic hence Headteachers should explore new approaches to strategic public management. Murray advocates for the HR approaches "which include decentralization, devolution and strategic planning" (p.118). The Headteachers will need to practice Ulrich's (2008) ten aspects which have innovative perspective leading to value creation. The value addition to the school will buffer the quality of education and enhance the Headteachers' transfer of skills. Murray warns that as values are created, the bedrock values should not be damaged. Therefore the Headteachers should be sensible broadly and keep track of the performance in all sections of the school. The Headteachers should embrace innovative HR roles.

The final approach to overcome the challenge was motivation. The Headteachers dealt with the basic requirement of a human being motivation. Several approaches were used to motivate the teachers from words of encouragement, handouts or scenarios which motivated the teachers. The approach is in congruence with Barczak, MeDonough and Athanassiou who recommend that the Headteachers should try to understand the teacher motivation.

The Headteachers did not realize that effective transfer of ELMT skills is interconnected, collaborative and involves context and content. Stacey (2003) urges the Headteachers to adopt new methodologies of inquiry in studying the process of ELMT skills transfer. Cicmil (2003) observes that knowledge is often assumed to exist independently of the context and the possibility of its capturing and codification is taken for granted. On the contrary, power to create knowledge is not just with the Headteachers but also in the interaction with others and the environment. Therefore the Headteachers should encourage collaboration and strong communication among teaching team members so as to perform better (Yazici, 2009). Stacey advices the Headteachers to appreciate that knowledge and learning are context dependent and are 'performed', actualized in conversations and other types of communication that involve individual and group relating in the medium of symbols, artifacts and power relations.

Headteachers need to be more aware of entrepreneurial orientations (EO) which are processes, structures and behaviors of schools that are characterized by five dimensions namely: autonomy, innovativeness, risk taking, proactiveness, and competitive aggressiveness (Lumpkin & Dess, 1996). The orientation will empower the Headteachers in addressing the barriers faced during the ELMT skill transfer. The dimensions will enable the Headteachers to make decisions, come up with innovative ideas, implement them by being proactive and engaging the most competitive team members. Headteachers need to be innovative as they improve their school governance based on novel ideas (Burbiel, 2009). EO develops new routines, competencies, and technologies and therefore need networks rich in bridging ties for new combinations of productive factors (Low & Abrahamson, 1997).

Despite the Headteachers being exposed to new ideas, many tried to implement the new ideas while working in the old ways. Readon and McLaughlin (2008) caution this approach as the Headteachers and the teachers must change the way they work for comprehensive outcome. The Headteachers should have the ability to influence organizational norms, conduct influenced decisions, determine the level of quality communication, buy-in and cooperation (Nada, Andrew, & Lee-Davies, 2008). For example the Headteachers did not explore the use of technology to support their transfer of ELMT skills. Utility of IT will facilitate gaining insight, both internally and externally hence facilitating school learning. According to Cho, Ozment, and Sink (2008) learning orientation could be linked to the school performance. Headteachers must strategically use IT to provide the relevant information to appropriate individuals or team depending on the needs at specific times (Tsai & Hung, 2008). IT utility in school governance will facilitate the acquisition and spreading of information (Hirose and Sonehara, 2008). According to Senge (1990) the Headteachers should explore system thinking facilitated by IT to involve interrelationship and connectivity aspects which include, knowing what other parts of the subject panels are doing and making decisions to complement their activities. The Headteachers will need to infuse the responsible use of technology as on the contrary the impact could be negative (Hirose & Sonara, 2008, Ito & Kagaya, 2006, Senge, 1990).

In spite of the Headteachers doing the strategic planning, they did not implement the approach on their transfer of ELMT skills. According to Gratton (2007) and Willington (2001), the Headteachers should embrace evolutionary approach to strategy which is based on the view that schools operate within the changing economic environments, need to respond for summary and effectiveness. The challenges are contextual and Hofstede (1988) recommends the inclusion of cultural contexts that will bring many players with various opinions and approaches to strategy development. As much as the Headteachers are exposed to strategic planning, they should also be informed of the possibilities of using the same approaches towards their plan of transfer of the ELMT skills.

The Headteachers did not consider the transfer of skills as a project. Despite learning the strategic plan they started embracing new approaches to school governance as part of the new way of working without considering it as a project. The consideration of the transfer as a project will have allowed the Headteachers to assign capable members to the transfer of skills team's (Smith and Reinerstein, 1992). Burkat (1994), Damanpour (1991), Kerzner (2009) and Zhead Heady (1994) advices the Headteachers to argument touting the benefits of selecting team members with training and self-esteem, broad based competences, high professionalism and full time commitment. The advice is plausible. However, there could be a possibility that that the teachers in the school do not fit such profiles. Nevertheless, the Headteachers should try since human asserts both individually and at organizational level play a key role in success (Bamay and Wright, 1988) The project view of transfer of skills will mean that the school performance will be based on how well the school is able to transfer and apply knowledge in an effective and efficient manner (Spender & Grant, 1996).

Although the Headteachers cited resources as a barrier, they never mentioned competency skill on financial management as a barrier. With the FPE, the Headteachers have become accounting managers. To enhance school governance, the Headteachers need to understand the inaccuracies in the current accounting systems, and explore opportunities for involving their teachers. According to Stewart (2002) books do not represent the actual situation but rather the required states. On the other hand the books are utilized specifically by different stakeholders. The Headteachers need to realize that the multiplicity of representation leads to lack of reality hence it impacts on decision making especially on the doctored reports.

The Headteachers should be aware that it is erroneous to associate financial sources with investment uses (Stern Stewart Research Evaluation., 2002, September). Stewart outlines that "failure to align accounting principle to economic values [will force Headteachers] to live in two worlds" p. 6. The dual situation is very dicey as single decisions cannot be sustained in twin forked conditions. The economic measures as suggested by Stewart will be the best approach because they are stable. Stewart (2002) observes that "debt exaggerates the apparent payoff which a [school] earns from its investments" (p. 5). Stewart warns that that Headteachers might be tempted, while handling bad debts to provide a cushion for lean times. The provision of the bad debt reserve, does not provide accurate information because the bad debts are estimates in the event of payment, the money could be used for "smoothing reported earnings and stabilizing bonuses" (Stewart, p. 17). The prediction of bad debt is usually a probability and it is important for the Headteachers to take precaution and put up intervention measures as they have done currently. However what they do with the payment needs to be tracked so that risks are contained. A key issue on loans is the pre-booked losses vs. pre-recorded grossed up interest on paid loans, Stewart (2002). According to Stewart accountants usually prefer the latter because of the benefit of doubt. The benefit of doubt is biased as it only considers one side.

Headteachers should be aware that intangibles are not recognized as realistic assets by the current practice yet they are important in spearheading development and new products. According to the TSC, performance contracts have been introduced in the schools, hence ELMT should be reviewed to enable the Headteachers to bridge the transfer gap if they are able to understand Activity Based Costing (ABC), the Balanced Scorecard (BSC) and EVA which are modern tools for performance measurements and management (Schinder & McDowell, 1999). The decision on which tool(s) to use depends on the knowledge of whether the tools are mutually exclusive or can be used together. Factors should according to Dror (2008), be considered when analyzing organizational performance management tools. The analysis of each framework according to Utley's (1999) cited in Dror (2008) suggestions, offers informed choice on making preferences to cope with the current trends and competition hence delivering value.

The Headteachers had gone through a unit on technology integration in school leadership. However, during their responses on overcoming the barrier, technology was not cited at all. The skills the Headteachers had acquired during the ELMT could be utilized to use technology for both individual learning and school learning. According to Senge (1990), to gain insight several mental models must be used to interpret the perception and information. Headteachers' exploitation will offer pillars that might facilitate the learning. According to Cho Ozment and Sink (2008) learning orientation could be linked to school performance. Furthermore the internet provides dynamic medium for channeling information between schools hence networking the Headteachers (Banduchi, 2005). The Headteachers will have opportunities to strategically use IT to provide relevant information for appropriate individuals or teams depending on the needs at specific times (Tsai & Hung, 2008). Therefore the IT utility in school governance will facilitate the acquisition and spreading of information (Hirose and Sonehara, 2008). The exploration of using technology will enhance community to facilitate learning and networking. There is need to establish effective utility of IT during the training so that the Headteachers are able to see the benefit during and after the course.

Conclusions and Practical Recommendations

In the study the first question aimed at the ELMT skills. These levels of implementation were looked through leadership, teams and networking. Transformational leadership by the Headteacher was well distributed with dominance on one style but varied depending on the tasks and preferences of the Headteachers. The Headteacher leadership influenced their outlook on their pedagogical leadership. The Headteachers had challenges in handling teams. The nurturing or the provision of positive aspects in the team was used to facilitate the success of the team to overcome the challenges. The Headteacher appreciated the government's role especially in quality assurance and professional learning however they felt that the support needed to be more. Lack of support or involvement from BOM and PTA in school activities was an indicator that the Headteachers were struggling with this part of networking. The fact that the handicap was on school involvement and support could be an indicator of decline.

Most of the implemented skills were on managing resources and pedagogical leadership at equal levels. Other implemented skills in the order of implementation levels were action research, emerging issues, guidance and counseling, reflective practice, and networking. A deeper analysis brought out understanding of 55% of the ELMT topics which corresponded with a 55% implementation of all ELMT topics. There was no correlation between understanding a topic and its implementation. However, cumulatively there was a relationship between the understanding of the topic and its implementation. A practical recommendation will be that effort could be made in all trainings to ensure that the level of understanding of the topics is either excellent or good. This is because there will be a relationship between understanding at these levels and effective implementation. Implementation structures should be put in place so that the level of understanding can be tracked with the training and efforts are made for remedial so that the gaps can be filled before the training is completed, this will ensure most or majority of the Headteachers attending the training have either understood at excellent levels or at good levels. The levels of implementation were influenced by the levels of understanding of the concepts. The Headteachers attempted to implement, what they had a good or fair understanding on a frequency of occasional or always. The level of implementation can be confirmed to be slightly above half of the topics that were covered but with strengths in specific areas where they are not facing barriers or were able to tame or manage the barriers.

The second question was looking the Headteachers perspective on barriers. These include the Headteachers' perspective on Newstrom's barriers, their action before, during and after ELMT, their organizational structures and preferred behavioral models and the barriers they identified. The actions of the Headteachers before the training influenced the level of preparedness and how motivated the Headteachers were. The Headteachers were partially ready for ELMT based on their actions before the course. However this cannot be only the Headteachers' responsibility but also the responsibility of the organizers of the ELMT programmes. Some of the practical recommendations here could include that the organizers of the ELMT design activities that could trigger the actions of the Headteacher before the training. The transfer of skills in training is influenced by what the trainees do before the training. However the responsibilities of these activities will involve both the participants attending the training as well as the organizers of the training both of these have the role of ensuring that the activities before the training are done to ensure transfer of skills. During the training the actions were dependent on course design and the Headteachers themselves. A practical recommendation will be the course designers to be aware of the actions required during the training and create an environment where the actions can be enacted. It will be important for the facilitators to implore on the participants and to ensure they act the roles they are supposed to do. The levels of ELMT training implementation after the training correlate to the action of the Headteachers during the training. The post ELMT actions were mainly in the core and support structure as well as independent disposition hence a practical application will be for the stakeholder that is the course organizers, the Headteachers and their managers should be able to understand the required action after the training so that they facilitate these actions. Therefore the actions before, during and after ELMT involve the course designers, the Headteachers and the managers so as to be able to overcome or manage the barriers to transfer of training. Schools, therefore, need to consider Headteachers' perceptions of the work environment when implementing methods to enhance transfer; before spending the added investment on innovative post training interventions, it is imperative that managers first assess and improve Headteachers' perceptions of the supportiveness of the work environment.

The managers were seen as the key organizational support; hence the MoEST and TSC who demand for the Headteacher to attain PLS should be aware of their key responsibility its potential impact in their transfer of ELMT. MoEST's and TSC's realization of their responsibility not only sending teachers for ELMT but providing support to remove the blame game where Headteacher have been accused of not implementing what they have learnt. The organizational behavior referred by the Headteachers is where all teachers were actively involved and were committed to the performance of the school. Elements of teams and efforts were core in the organizational behavior referred by the Headteacher. All the schools were on transition and had no predominant behavior mode.

Newstrom ranking can be influenced by the Headteachers preferences and perspectives on barriers therefore rankings cannot be generalized or considered for the impact of barriers and ELMT transfer of practice. Newstrom had uncategorized aspects that were considered primary impact by the Headteacher. Newstrom categorized aspects were considered primary aspects by the Headteacher. The Headteacher were more concerned with support from managers and the environment they are working in during the training. The similarities between Newstrom's category and the Headteachers were only 2 barriers out of 9 identified barriers.

The Headteachers identified six barriers to transfer of ELMT transfer of skills. The barriers were teachers, resources, policy, culture support and students. From these barriers it is clear that the policies that safe guard the availability of finite resources so as to have an accommodating working environment beneficial to schools. There should be clear policies that guide the school to realize their goals without harm while being aligned to government. As teachers were found to be the peer barriers it is important to explore ways in which teachers can be treated equally and in a nurturing way such that peer support can be natured through different approaches.

It has been identified that barriers can be influenced by the activities of the ELMT training, therefore it is important that information is provided to the Headteachers before ELMT by the organizers and it needs to be comprehensive to allow the Headteachers to have level of preparedness which is apt. Secondly participation during ELMT should be enhanced through the designs, the passion and commitment of the Headteacher. These two aspects will need the organizers input in terms of designing and of the communication the information to the Headteachers so as they can be able to ignite the motivation and interest to attend and actively participate in ELMT.

The Headteacher developed their approaches for managing and overcoming barriers. Some of these approaches could be supported by the business management skills to make them more effective. Additionally there were other business management skills which could be used further to increase the approaches of overcoming and managing the barriers. The Headteacher's approaches included

-   Overcoming fear.
-   Appreciating change.
-   Seeking support from the peers.
-   Utilizing the support from their manager.

- Exploiting stakeholders
- Building teams
- Effectively managing resources.
- Motivating the teachers.

These approaches gained some grounds in overcoming the barriers but they were not adequate based on the level of performance or the expected improvement in NEP trends. The approaches could be supplemented by several business management skills. Managing hot spots was one approach that could assist the Headteacher. The focus on the vital few will help the Headteachers in terms of identifying the vital few and the trivial many. The seeking of peer support through mentoring and shadowing will empower the Headteacher in overcoming the barriers. The utility of the team concepts will increase the people involved in the transfer and therefore enhance the support within the school through networking and across other schools through networking. The implementation of the advocated organizational behavior will influence the preferred behavioral model which will be adequate in terms of influencing the barriers.

Managing the scarce resources was an approach the Headteachers used to tame the challenges from the business management. The Headteacher could tap the concept of outsourcing and teachers' management through innovative human resource practices and their abilities to stating and fully utilizing the tools at their disposal, this will assist the Headteachers in addressing the issue of managing resources. These are the approaches the Headteachers implemented in overcoming the barriers and the suggested business management concepts which could be supplemented to support the Headteachers in their current approach of overcoming the barriers. However there are other business concepts which could be utilized although they were not identified or related to the Headteachers approaches.

Such approaches will include understanding the concepts that the transfer of ELMT skills is interconnected, collaborative and involves context and content. The aspect of entrepreneurial evaluation will facilitate in overcoming the barriers. The utility of technology will assist the Headteacher in reaching out as well as accessing information that will be useful. The Headteacher should embrace strategic planning. in their transfer of ELMT skills so as to have a competitive advantage as well as be able to monitor their progress. There is need for the Headteacher to embrace the transfer of ELMT skills as a project, this will allow them to infuse earned value project and process management to overcome barrier. With FPE the Headteachers will need EVA, BSC and ABC as they will help them on performance management tracking.

The Headteacher had their ingenious way of overcoming the barriers. However that was not adequate. The Headteacher needed supplementary skills to support their approaches and additional skills to respond to the areas they either did not identify or were not aware. Hence there is need for the course organizers to explore and identify ways in which they can infuse the business management concepts to upscale the Headteacher in overcoming the barriers. Caution should be exercised because it has been noted that it's not only the content that will empower the Headteacher but also the process before during and after ELMT. There should be a holistic view in the review that will address the interconnectedness and the contextual experiences.

Recommendations for Further Research

This research brought out findings which indicated a need for further research in the areas of skills, understanding and transfers matching, teachers experiences in the transfer of skills initiated by the Headteachers, how the successfully transferred skills were presented to the Headteachers during training and the extent in which the business skills were applicable or could be applicable to overcome the barriers.

One of the areas for future research is to be able to identify how the Headteachers decided which topic to begin with and to implement. When Headteachers graduated they had around thirty two concepts which they were exposed to over six months when there is need to understand how they decided, which topic to implement. What informed them on which topics to implement and how did they make the decisions?

The second aspect on future research is on financial management. The Headteachers under FPE received money to run schools. There is need to know how they have been managing their finances and how the aspect of financing management was affecting or influencing the performance of the schools. How does financial management influence the performance of schools under FPE?

The third aspect for future research is on action research. There is need to explore and identify how the Headteachers selected the action research topics and the impact of the finding of this action research, each topic had in the performance of the school its important because the Headteachers were exposed to action research skills. There is need to know the effectiveness and the impact the action research had had towards the performance of the students in the school.

There is need to explore the percentage of failure in implementing the ELMT skills and the reasons for the failure. As a fourth recommendation it will give insights as to the root causes of the failure and explore ways of overcoming the failures. Furthermore there is also need to establish the support mechanism after training a detailed exploration of what support is offered as physical, financial and human resource will establish a deeper understanding of the nature of support and the level of support that the Headteacher receives after the ELMT training.

Although this research explored the level of transfer of skills in NEP improving schools there is a need to explore all the participants and identify the percentage of implementation without linking it to the NEP trends. This fifth recommendation will be purely be addressing the percentage implementers without linking it to the NEP trends.

The study looked at the level of implementation and it established a cumulative relationship between understanding and implementation. A sixth recommendation will be to research on itemized relationship by exploring how the individual topics were related in terms of understanding and implementation. The topical analysis of understanding and implementation will provide a clearer relationship between the two aspects of level of understanding and implementation. These are the six aspects that need to be researched on further so as to understand in depth the transfer of EMLT into school governance.

References

Abella, R. S. (1985). *Equality in Employement: A Rotal Commision Report: Research Studies.* Ottawa: Canadian Government Publishing Center.

Agriteam Canada. (2013). *SESEA Baseline Tools-Partnership for Advancing Human Development in Africa and Asia.* Calgary, CA: AGRITEAM CANADA CONSULTING LTD.

AKAM. (2013). *Educational Leadership and Managment Course Handbook.* Aga Khan Academy, Mombasa, Professional Development Center. Mombasa: Aga Khan Academy.

AKFC. (2011). *Strenghthening Education Systems in East Africa: Proposed strategic direction and framework for DFATD-AKDN project.* Canada: Aga Khan Foundation.

Allen, S. J. (2007). Adult learning theory and leadership development. *Leadership Review, 7,* 26–37.

Alvarez, K., Salas, E., & Garofano, C. M. (2004). An integrated model of training evaluation and effectiveness. *Human Resource Development Review, 3*(4), 385–416.

Anne, D. (1993). Cross-functional teams in product development: Accommodating the structure to the process. *Journal of Productivity Innovation Management, 10,* 377-392.

Argyris, C. (1995). Action science and organizational learning. *Journal of Managerial Psychology, 10,* 20–26.

Aucoin, P. (1991). *Internalizing the Vendor's Resources: Outsourcing in the 1990s.* Carrollton, TX:: Chantico Publishing Co., Inc.

Avolio, B. J., Avey, J. B., & Quisenberry, D. (2010). Estimating return on leadership development investment. *The Leadership Quarterly, 21,* 633–644.

Avolio, B. J., Reichard, R. J., Hannah, S. T., Walumbwa, F. O., & Chan, A. (2009.). Meta-analytic review of leadership impact: Experimental and quasi-experimental studies. *The Leadership Quarterly, 20,* 764–784.

Baldwin, T. T., & Ford, J. K. (1988). Transfer of training: A review and directions for future research. *Personnel Psychology, 41,* 63-105.

Baldwin-Evans, K. (2006). Key steps to implementing a successful blended learning strategy. . *Industrial & Commercial Training, 38,* 156–163.

Barczak, G., MeDonough, E. F., & Athanassiou, N. (2006). So you want to be a global project leader? *Research Technology Management, 49*(3), 28-35.

Barney, J. B., & Wright, P. M. (1988, Spring). On becoming a strategic partner: The role of human resources in gaining competitive advantage. *Human Resource Management,* 31-46.

Bass, B. M., Jung, D. I., Avolio, B. J., & Berson, Y. (2003). Predicting Unit performance by assessing tranformational and transactional leadership. *Journal of Applied Psychology, 88*(2), 207-218.

Bassey, M. (1999). *Case study research in educational setting.* . Philadelphia: Open University.

Bates, R. A. (2003). Managers as transfer agents: Improving learning transfer in organizations. In E. F. Holton, & T. T. Baldwin, *Improving learning transfer in organizations* (pp. 243–270). San Francisco: Jossey-Bass.

Belassi, W., Kondra, A. Z., & Tukel, O. I. (2007). New product development projects: the effects of organizational culture. *Project Management Journal, 38*(4), 12-24.

Bernie, J. (1990). *Neighborhood Planning: A Guide for Citizens and Planners.* Chicago and Washington, D.C.: Planners Press, American Planning Association.

Birdi, K., Allan, C., & Warr, P. (1997). Correlates of perceived outcomes of four types of employee development activity. 82,. *Journal of Applied Psychology, 82,* 845–857.

Blednick, J., & Wilson, G. L. (2011). *Teaching in Tandem: Co-teaching in the inclusive classroom.* Alexandria, USA: ASCD.

Blumberg, Cooper, P., & Schindler, D. (2008). *Business Research Methods.* New York, NY: McGraw-Hill.

Bowman, C., & Schoenberg, R. (2008). From Customer understanding to Strategy Innovation: Practical Tools to Establish Competative Positioning. In R. Galavan, J. Markides, & C. Murray, *Strategy, Innovation and Change: Challenges in management* (pp. 38-56). Oxford: OUP.

Boyatzis, R. E. (1998). *Transforming qualitative information. Thematic analysis and code development.* . Thousand Oaks, CA: Sage Publications.

Breakwell, G. M., Hammond, S., Fife-Schaw, C., & Smith, J. A. (2006). *Research methods in psychology* (3 rd ed.). London: Sage.

Brewster, P., & Chandra, G. (1999). Economic Value Added (EVA): Its uses and limitation. *SAM Advanced Management Journal, 64*(2), 1-12.

Broad, M. L. (2002). *Beyond Tranfer of Training: Engaging Systems to imporve performance.* . CA: John Wiley & Sons.

Broad, M. L., & Newstrom, J. W. (1992). *Transfer of training: Action-packed strategies to ensure high payoff from training investments.* Cambridge, England: Perseus.

Brown, K. G., & Ford, J. K. (2002). Technology in training: Building an infrastructure for active learning. In K. Kraiger, *Creating, implementing, and managing effective training and development: State-of-the-art lessons for practice.* (p. 192–233). San Francisco, CA: Jossey-Bass.

Burbiel, J. (2009). Creativity in reserach and development environment: A practical review. International Journal of Business Science and Applied Management. *4*(2), 35-51.

Burgess, D. (2005). What motivates employees to transfer knowledge outside their work unit? *Journal of Business Communication., 42,* 324—348.

Burkat, R. E. (1994). Reducing R& D cycle time. *Research technology management., 37,* 27-31.

Burke, L. A., & Baldwin, T. (1999b). Workforce training transfer: A study of the effect of relapse prevention and transfer climate. *Human Resource Management, 38*(3), 227-242.

Burke, L. A., & Hutchins, H. M. (2008). A study of best practices in training transfer and proposed model for transfer. *Human Resource Development Quarterly, 19*(2), 107-128.

Burke, L., & Baldwin, T. (1999a). *First break all the rules: What the world's greatest managers do differently.* New York, NY: Simon & Schuster.

Cheng, E., & Hampson, I. (2008). Transfer and training: A review and new insights. *International Journal of Management Reviews, 10*(4), 327-341.

Chin, H. G. (2011). *Sustaining the Transfer of Learning beyond Leadership Development Programmes.* Retrieved December 12, 2013, from Civil Service College: http://www.cscollege.gov.sg/Knowledge/Pages/Sustaining-the-Transfer-of-Learning-beyond-Leadership-Development-Programmes.aspx#notes

Cicmil, S. (2003). Knowledge, Interaction, and Project Work: From Instrumental Rationality to practical wisdom. Leicester, UK: De Moft University.

Clark, D. (2013). *The Art and Science of Leadership.* Retrieved June 30, 2013, from A Timeline of Managment and Leadership.: http://nwlink.com/-donclark/leader/leadtrn.html

Clarke, N. (2004). HRD and the challenges of assessing learning in the workplace. *International Journal of Training and Development, 8,* 140–156.

Clarke, N. (2005). Workplace learning environment and its relationship with learning outcomes in healthcare organizations. *Human Resource Development International, 8*(2), 185-205.

Clegg, S. R., & Hardy, C. (1996). Organizations, organization and organizing. In S. R. Clegg, C. Hardy, & W. Nord, *Handbook of organizational studies* (pp. 1-28). Thousand Oaks, CA: Sage Publications.

Cleland, D. I., & King, W. R. (1983). *Systems analysis and project management.* NewYork: McGraw-Hill.

Coates, D. E. (2007). Info line. *Enhance the training of training: Tips, Tools and Intelligence for Trainers, 0710.* (J. Brusino, Ed.) USA: ASTD.

Cohen, L., & Manion, L. (2000). *Research methods in education.* London: Routledge Falmer.

Colquitt, J., LePine, J., & Noe, R. (2000). Toward an integrative theory of training motivation: A meta-analytic path analysis of 20 years of research. *Journal of Applied Psychology, 85*(5), 678-707.

Cresswell, J. (2003). *Research design: Quantitative and mixed mode approaches.* United Kingdom: Sage.

Creswell, J. W. (2007). *Qualitative inquiry and research design: choosing among five approaches.* Unites States of America: Sage.

Creswell, J. W. (2008). *Educational Research: Planning, conducting and evaluating quantitative and qualitative research.* Columbus, OH: Prentice Hall.

Crew, R. (2007). *Only Connect: The way to save our schools.* New York, NY: Sarah Crichton Books.

Cromwell, S. E., & Kolb, J. A. (2004). An examination of work-environment support factors affecting transfer of supervisory skills training to the workplace. *Human Resource Development Quarterly, 15*(4), 449-471.

Damanpour, F. (1991). Organizational innovation: A meta – analysis of effects of determinants and moderators. *Academy of Management Journal, 34,* 555- 590.

Dartey-Baah, K., & Amoako, G. K. (2011). Application of Frederick Herzberg's Two-Factor theory in assessing and understanding employee motivation at work: a Ghanaian Perspective. *European Journal of Business and Management, 3*(9), 1-9.

Denzin, N. K., & Lincoln, Y. S. (1994). *Handbook of qualitative research.* . Newbury Park, CA: Sage.

Dror, S. (2008). The Balanced Scorecard Versus quality award models as strategic framework. *Total Quality Managemnet, 19*(6), 583-593.

Drucker, P. F. (1995). The Information Executives truly need. . *Harvard Business Review,* 54-62.

Eskerod, P., & Skriver, P. (2007). Organizational culture restraining in – house knowledge transfer between project managers - A case study. *Project management journal, 38*(1), 110- 122.

Facteau, J., Dobbins, G., Russel, J., Ladd, R., & Kudisch, J. (1995). The influence of general perceptions of the training environment on pretraining motivation and perceived training transfer. *Journal of Management, 21*(1), 1-25.

Freeman, R., & Rogers, J. (1999). *What Workers Want. Ithaca.* NY: ILR Press.

Gay, L., & Airasian, P. (2000). *Educational research: competencies for analysis and application.* New Jersey: Prentice Hall.

Gioko, A. (2011). *Certificate in educational leadership and management Program Report (Phase 1).* Mombasa: Aga Khan University.

Gioko, A. M. (2013). Creating an effective professional learning sessions model on technology integration for a Kenyan school district. . *Education and Information Technologies., 18*(2), 151-164.

Gioko, M. A. (2007). *Science Subject Leadership In The Enhancement Of Information Communication Technology (ICT) Integration In Project Based Learning (PBL) In A Private Secondary School In Pakistan.* Unpublished master's thesis., Aga Khan University, Karachi, Pakistan.

Gist, M., Bavetta, A., & Steven, C. K. (1990). Transfer training method: Its influence on skill generalization, skill repetition, and performance level. *Personnel Psychology, 43*(3), 501.

Glassman, G., & Hopkins, K. (1984). *Statistical methods in education and psychology.* Englewood Cliffs, NJ: Prentice Hall.

Glesne, C. (1999). *Becoming qualitative researcher.* U.S.A.: Longman.

Gobeli, D., Koenig, H. F., & Bechinger, H. (1998). Managing conflict in software development team multi-level analysis. *Journal of Product Innovation Management, 15*, 423—435.

Goldstein, I. L. (1986). *Training in organizations: Needs assessment, design, and evaluation.* . Monterey, CA: Brooks/Cole.

Gratton, L. (2007). *Hot Spots: Why Some Teams, Workplaces, and Organisations Buzz with Energy and others Dont.* . San Franscisco: BarrettKoekler Publisher.

Gresham, G., Hafer, J., & & Markowski, E. (2006). Inter-fuctional market orientation between ing departments and technical departments in management of new products. *Journal of behavioral and Applied Management, 81*(1), 343-365.

Griffin, A., & Page, A. L. (1996). PDMA successes measurement project. Recommended measures for product development success and failure. *Journal of product innovative management*, 478- 496.

Griffith, G., & Allen, L. (2012, July 04). *Transfer of Training. How to Help your staff Translate what they Learn into what they do.* Retrieved July 3, 2013, from Slideshare: http://www.slideshare.net/gailgriff/transfer-of-training-13541475

Grisham, T. W. (2010). *International Project Management: Leadership in Complex environments.* New Jersey: John Wiley & Sons.

Gupta, V. K., & Moesel, D. M. (2007). The impact of entrepreneurial orientation on knowledge management in strategic alliances: Evidence from high-technology SMEs. *Annual USASBE Conference.* Florida.

Gurbuz, G., & Aykol, S. (2009). Entrepreneurial management, entrepreneurial orientation and Turkish small firm growth. *Management Research News, 32*(4), 321-336.

Hammersley-Fletcher, L. &. (2004). Evaluating our peers: is peer observation a meaningful ingful process? . *Studies in Higher Education, 29*(4), 489–503.

Hannah, S. T., & Lester, P. B. (2009). A multilevel approach to building and leading learning organisations. *The Leadership Quarterly, 20*, 34-48.

Hannum, K. M., Martineau, J. W., & Reinelt, C. (2007). *The handbook of leadership development evaluation.* San Francisco, CA: Jossey-Bass.

Harris, S. G., & Cole, M. S. (2007). A stages of change perspective on managers' motivation to learn in a leadership development context. 20,. *Journal of Organisational Change Management, 20*, 774–793.

Hawley, J. D., & Barnard, J. K. (2005). Work environment characteristics and implications for training transfer: A case study of the nuclear power industry. *Human Resource Development International, 8*(1), 65–80.

Hayashi, A. M. (2004). Building better teams. *MIT Sloan Management Review*, 5.

Hayek, F. A. (1937). Economic and Knowledge. Economica. *New Series, 4*(13), 33-54.

Henning, E., Van Rensburg, W., & Smith, B. (2004). *Finding your way in qualitative research.* Pretoria: Van Schaik.

Hirose, Y., & Sonehara, N. (2008). Management of inofrmation credibility risk in an ICT society. *Internet Research, 18*(2), 142-154.

Hofstede, G. H. (1988). *Culture's Consequence.* . Beverly Hills, US: Sage.

Holton, V., Voller, S., Schofield, C., & Devine, M. (2010). *Improving learning transfer: A pilot study with three Ashridge client organisations [Ashridge Report].* Retrieved December 30, 2013, from http://www.ashridge:

http://www.ashridgeleadershipcentre.com/website/IC.nsf/wFARATT/Improving%20learning%20
    transfer/$file/ImprovingLearningTransfer.pdf

Honey, M., & Culp, M. K. (2005). *Critical Issue: Using Technology to Improve Student Achievement.* Retrieved
    Novermber 11, 2014, from North Central Regional Education Laboratory: http://www.ncrel.org/sdrs/areas/
    issues/methods/technlgy/te800.htm

Hong, M., Hahm, A. Y., & Doll, W. J. (2004). The role of project target clarity in an uncertain project
    environment. *International Journal of Operations & Production Management., 24,* 1269-1291.

Hunter-Johnson, Y. (2013). When Training Is Not Enough: An Appeal to the Work Environment for Transfer
    of Training in the Bahamian Police Force. *The international Journal of Bahamian Studies, 19,* 3-14.

Hunter-Johnson, Y., & Closson, R. (2011). From the shooting range tothe street: Training facilitators' perception
    on transfer of training. *American Association for Adult and Continuing Educatio.* Indianapolis, Indiana.

Ito, K., & Kagaya, T. (2006). Brand risk management and cooporate value. . *Hitosubashi Business Review.*

Jeffrey, R., Michael, X., & Shin, G. C. (2003.). Project management characteristics and new product survival.
    Journal of Product Innovation Management., 20(2), 104—119.

Johnson, R. B., & Christensen, L. B. (2008). *Educational research: Quantitative and Qualitative approaches.* (3
    rd ed.). Thousand Oaks CA: Sage.

Jorgensen, B., & Emmitt, S. (2009). Investigating the integration of design and construction from a lean
    perspective. *Journal of Construction Innovation, 9*(2), 225-240.

Jungalwalla, R. (2000). Transforming Groups into Teams. *Executive Excellence, 17* (2).

Kaizenbach, J. R., & Douglas, K. S. (1993). *The Wisdom of Teams: Creating the High-Performance Organization.*
    Boston: Harvard Business School Press.

Kaler, J. (2003). Differentiating Stakeholder Theories. *Journal of Business Ethics, 46*(1/2), 71–83.

Kanter, R. M. (1983). *The change masters: innovation and entreprenuership in the American corporation.* New
    York: Simon & Schuster.

Kaplan, R. S., & Norton, D. P. (1996, January-February). Using the Balanced Scorecard as a Strategic
    Management System. pp. 1-13.

Kerzner, H. (2009). *Project Managment: A system Approach to Planning, Scheduling, and Controlling.* John Willey
    & Sons, Inc.

KNEC. (2013). *2012 KCPE Examination Essential Statistics.* Nairobi: Kenya Examination Council.

Kozlowski, S., & Salas, E. (1997). A multilevel organizational systems approach for the implementation and
    transfer of training. In S. K. J. K. Ford, *Improving training effectiveness in work organizations* (pp. 247-287).
    New Jersey: Erlbaum.

Kropp, F., Lindsay, N., & Shoham, A. (2008). Entrepreneurial orientation and international entrepreneurial
    business venture startup. *International Journal of Entrepreneurial Behavior and Research, 14*(2), 102-117.

Kvale, S. (1996). *Interviewing in Sociology.* . U.S.A.: Sage publications.

Lammers, M., & Tsretko, N. (2008). *More with less the 80/20 rule of PM.* Retrieved June 17,
    2013, from http://web.ebscohost.com/ehost/pdfviewer/pdfviewer?vid=5&hid=11&sid=8e14
    99a7-f379-4151-9773-31a349cb0605%40sessionmgr11

Latham, G., Millman, Z., & Miedema, H. (1998). Theoretical, practical and organizational issues affecting
    training. In P. Drenth, H. Theirry, & C. deWolff, *Personnel Psychology* (pp. 1-25). East Sussex: Psychology
    Press.

Leimbach, M. (2010). Learning transfer model: A research-driven approach to enhancing learning effectiveness.
    Industrial and Commercial Training, 42, 81–86.

Lett, J. (1990). Emics and etics: Notes on the epistemology of anthropology. In K. P. In T.N. Headland, *Emics and etics: The insider/outsider debate. Frontiers of anthropology.* (Vol. 7). Newbury Park, Calif: Sage Publications.

Lewis, M. W., Welsh, M. A., Dehler, G. E., & Green, S. G. (2002). Product development tensions: Exploring contrasting styles of project management. *Academy of Management Journal, 45*(3), 546-564.

Lewis, P. J. (1993). *How to Build and Manage a Winning Project Team.* New York: American Management Association.

Liebermann, S., & Hoffmann, S. (2008). The impact of practical relevance on training transfer: evidence from a service quality-training program for German bank clerks. . *International Journal of Training and Development, 12*(2), 74-76.

Lincoln, Y. S., & Guba, E. G. (2000). The only generalization is: There is no generalization. In M. H. Gomm, *EdsCase study method, key issues, key texts.* (pp. 27-40). Thousand Oaks, CA: Sage.

Loh, L., & Venkatraman, N. .. (1992). *Stock market reaction to information technology outsourcing: An event study.* Alfred P. Working paper no. 3499-92BPS, Sloan School of Management.

Low, M. B., & Abrahamson, E. (1997). Movements, band- wagons, and clones: Industry evolution and the entrepreneurial process. *Journal of Business Venturing, 12*, 435– 457.

Lumpkin, G. T., & Dess, G. G. (1996). Clarifying the Entrepreneurial Orientation Construct and Linking It to Performance. *The Academy of Management Review, 21*(1), 135-172.

Lumpkin, G. T., & Dess, G. G. (2001). Linking two dimensions of entrepreneurial orientation to firm performance: moderating role of environment and industry life cycle. *Journal of Business Venturing, 16*, 429-451.

Marshal, C. &. (1999). *Designing qualitative research (3ʳᵈ ed.).* London, Thousand Oaks: Sage Publication.

Marshal, C., & Rossman, G. B. (1999). *Designing qualitative research* (3 rd ed.). London, Thousand Oaks: Sage Publication.

Mathieu, J. E., & Martineau, J. W. (1997). Individual and situational influences on training motivation. In J. K. Ford, S. W. Kozlowski, K. Kraiger, E. Salas, & M. S. Teachout, *Improving training effectiveness in work organisations.* New Jersey: Erlbaum.

Mawhinney, H. B. (1999). Reappraisal: The problems and prospects of studying the micro politics of leadership in reforming schools. *School Leadership & Management, 19*, 159-170.

McGee-Brown, M. J. (1994). *Teaching as a process of systematic interpretive inquiry: A phenomenological approach to teacher-directed research.* . Athens: The University of Georgia.

Meadows, A. K. (2003). So you want to do research? 4: An introduction to quantitative methods. *British Journal of community Nursing, 8*(11), 19-526.

Merriam, B. S. (1998a). *Case study research in education. A qualitative approach.* San Francisco, CA: Jossey-Bass.

Merriam, S. (1998b). *Case study research: A qualitative approach.* San Francisco: Jossey-Bass.

Miles, M. B., & Herberman, A. M. (1994). *Qualitative data analysis: An expanded source book.* (Eds ed.). California: Thousands Oaks.

Ministry of Education. (2008). The development of education, National report of Kenya Ministry of Education. *International conference on Education.* Geneva, Switzerland.

Morris, M. W., Leung, K., Ames, D., & Lickel, B. (1999). Views from inside and outside: Integrating Emic and Etic Insights about Culture and Justice Judgment. *Academy of Management Review, 24*(4), 781-796.

Moss, J. J., Jensrud, Q., & Johansen, B. C. (1992). *An evaluation of ten leadership development programs for graduate students in vocational education.* Berkeley, California.: National Center for Research in Vocational Education .

Murray, J. A. (2008). Services, Counsel, and Value: Managing Strategically in the Public Sector. . In R. Galavan, J. Markides, & C. Murray, *Strategy, innovation and Change: Challenges in Management* (pp. 111-128). Oxford: OUP.

Nada, K. K., Andrew, P. K., & Lee-Davies, L. (2008). The Contrasting Faces of the Chairman of the Board. In J. M. R. Galavan, & M. C., *Strategy, Innovation and Change: Challenges in Management* (pp. 242-253). Oxford: OUP.

Narveson, J. (2003). *Ethics in the Business and Professional Life.* Retrieved October 15, 2013, from http://swissmc. blackboard.com/webapps/blackboard/content/listContent.jsp?course_id=_307_1&content_id=_17024_1

Newstrom, J. W. (1986). Leveraging Management Development through the Management of Transfer. *Journal of Management Development, 5*(5), 33 - 45.

Nikoumaram, H., & Heidarzadeh, K. (2006). Evaluation the Role of Entrepreneurial Proctivity Organization Structure and Market Orientation on Business Performance. *Journal of Marketing's Management, 1*(0), 5-50.

Niven, P. R. (2002). *Balanced Scorecard Step-by-Step: Maximizing Performance and Mainating Results.* John Willey & Sons.

Noe, R. A., Hollenbeck, J. R., Gerhart, B., & & Wright, P. M. (2006). *Human resource management: Gaining a competitive advantage* (6th ed.). Boston, MA.

Noguera, P., & Wang, J. (2006). *Unfinished Business: Closing the racial achievement gap in our schools.* San Franscisco, CA: Jossey Bass.

Nugent, J. H. (2002). *Plan to Win: Analytical and Operational Tool-Gaining Competative Advantage.* McGraw-Hill.

Park, R., Appelbaum, E., & Kruse, D. (2010). Employee involvement and group incentives in manufacturing companies: a multi-level analysis. *Human Resource Management Journal, 20*(3), 227-243.

Patton, M. Q. (1990). *Qualitative evaluation methods.* Newbury Park: Sage.

Pfeiffer, J. (1994). *Competitive advantage through people.* Boston: Harvard Business press.

Pidd, K. (2002). Organisational barriers to training transfer: the role of workplace social controls and normative behaviour in workforce development. In *Catching clouds: Exploring diversity in workforce development for the alcohol and other drug field.* (pp. 135-144). Adelaide: National Centre for Education and Training on Addiction.

Pole, C., & Lampard, R. (2002). *Practical social investigation: qualitative and quantitative methods in social research.* Harlow, England: Prentice-hall.

Pons, D. (2008). Project Management for New Product Development. *Journal of Project Managment, 39*(2), 82-97.

Qu, W. G., Pinsonneault, A., & Oh, W. (2011). Influence of Industry Characteristics on Information Technology Outsourcing. . *Journal of Management Information Systems., 27*(4), 99–127.

Quinones, M. A. (1995). Pretraining context effects: Training assignment as feedback. *Journal of Applied Psychology, 80,* 226–238.

Quinones, M. A., Ford, J. K., Sego, D. J., & Smith, E. M. (1995). The effects of individual and transfer environment characteristics on the opportunity to performed trained tasks. *Training Research Journal, 1,* 29–48.

Readon, K., & McLaughlin, A. (2008). The Leaders as a Negotiator. In J. M. R. Galavan, & M. C., *Strategy, Innovation and Change: Challenges in Management* (pp. 281-296). Oxford: OUP.

Reh, J. F. (2005). *Pareto's Principle-the 80-20 rule.* Retrieved June 12, 2013, from http://web.ebscohost.com/ehost/pdfviewer/pdfviewer?sid=a9392bdf-ee01-4f2e-9c43-b7b0e1395abd%40sessionmgr11&vid=1&hid=13

Robinson, V. M. (2010). From instructional leadership to leadership capabilities: Empirical findings and methodological challenges. *Leadership and Policy in Schools, 9*(1), 1-26.

Robson, C. (2002). *Real World Research.* Cornwall: Blackwell Publishing.

Rossman, G., & Rallis, S. (1998). *Learning in the field: An introduction to qualitative research.* London: Sage Ltd.

Rouiler, J. Z., & Goldstein, I. L. (1993). The relationship between organizational transfer climate and positive transfer of training. *Human Resources Development Quarterly, 4*(4), 377-390.

Russon, C., & Reinelt, C. (2004). The results of an evaluation scan of 55 leadership development programs. *Journal of Leadership and Organizational Studies, 10,* 104–107.

Saks, A. M. (2002). So what is a good transfer of training estimate? A reply to Fitzpatrick. *The Industrial-Organizational Psychologist, 39*(3), 29-30.

Saks, A. M., & Belcourt, M. (2006). An investigation of training activities and transfer of training in organizations. . *Human Resource Management, 45,* 629–648.

Saunders, M., Lewis, P., & Thornhill, A. (2007). *Research Methods for Business Students* (4ᵗʰ ed.). England: Prentice Hall.

Schein, E. H. (1990). *Organisational, E.H. culture and leadership.* San Franscisco: Jossey- Bass.

Schinder, M.; McDowell, D. (1999). *ABC, The Balanced Scorecard and EVA Distinguishing the Means from the End.* Stern Stewart Research Evaluation, St George Street, London.

Schinder, M.; McDowell, D. (1999, April). ABC, The Balanced Scorecard and EVA Distinguishing the Means from the End. *1(2).* St George Street, London.

Scott, W. R. (1992). *Organizations: Rational, natural and open systems (3ʳᵈ ed.).* Englewood Cliffs. NJ: Prentice Hall.

Senge, P. M. (1990). *The fifth discipline: The art & practice of the learning organization..* New York: Doubleday.

Shepherd, M. (2004). Reflection on developing a reflective journal as a manager advisor. *Reflective Practice, 5*(2), 199-208.

Shinder, M., & McDowell, D. (1999). *ABC, The Balanced Score Card and EVA Distinguishing the Means from the End.* EVAluation.

Silverman, D. (2001). *Interpreting qualitative data: Methods for analysing talk, text and interaction* (2ⁿᵈ edition ed.). London: Sage.

SMCU. (2013). *Courses.* Retrieved November 21, 2013, from SMC University: http://swissmc.blackboard.com/webapps/portal/frameset.jsp?tab_tab_group_id=_1_1

Smith, P. G., & Reinertsen, D. G. (1992). Shortening th eproduct development cycle. *Reserach Technology Managment, 35,* 44-49.

Spender, J. C., & Grant, R. M. (1996). Knowledge and the firm: Overview. *Strategic Management Journal, 17,* 5–9.

Stacey, R. (2003). *Strategic Management and Organizational Dynamics-The Challenge of Complexity* (4ᵗʰ Ed ed.). Pearson: Harlow: FT Pretence Hall.

Stake, R. (1994). Case Studies. In N. D. Lincoln, *Handbook of quality research* (pp. 67-72). London:: Sage.

Stake, R. (1995). *The art of case study research .* Thousand Oaks: CA: Sage.

Stam, W., & Elfring, T. (2008). entrepreneurial orientation and new venture performance: the moderating role of intra- and extraindustry social capital. *Academy of Management Journal, 51*(1), 97-111.

Stern Stewart Research Evaluation. (2002, September). *Accounting Is Broken Here's How To Fix It: A Radical Manifesto.* New York: Stewart, B. C.

Stern, E.; Schönburg, J. (1999, June). The Capitalist Manifesto: The Transformation of a cooperation-Employee Capitalism. *Stern Stewart Research Evaluation, 1(4).* New York.

Stewart, G. B. (2002, September). Accounting Is Broken Here's How To Fix It: A Radical Manifesto. *Stewart Research Evaluation, 1(5).* New York.

Stoll, L., & Fink, D. (1996). *Changing our schools: Linking scholl effectiveness and school improvement.* Philadelphia: Open Press University.

Strauss, A. (1987). *Qualitative analysis for social scientists. .* Cambridge University Press.: Cambridge.

Strauss, A., & Corbin, J. (2007). *Basics of qualitative research. Techniques and procedures for developing grounded theory* (3rd ed.). Thousand Oaks, CA: Sage.

Suinn, R. (1990). *Psychological techniques for individual performance.* . New York: Macmillan.

Sun, T. (2009). *Mixed Methods Research: Strengths of two methods combined.* Retrieved March 31, 2011, from https://swissmc.blackboard.com/webapps/portal/frameset.jsp?tab_tab_group_id=_2_1&url=%2Fwebapps%2Fblackboard%2Fexecute%2Flauncher%3Ftype%3DCourse%26id%3D_104_1%26url%3D

Tappan, M. B. (2001). Interpretive psychology: Stories, circles, and understanding lived experience. In D. L. Brydon-Miller, *From Subjects to Subjectivities. A handbook of Interpretive and Participatory Methods* (pp. 45-56). New York: New York University Press.

Tracey, J., Hinkin, T., Tannenbaum, S., & Mathieu, J. (2001). The influence of individual characteristics and the work environment on varying levels of training outcomes. *Human Resource Development Quarterly, 12*(1), 5-22.

Tsai, W.-H., & Hung, S. J. (2008). E-Commerce Implementation: An Empirical Study of the Performance of Enterprise Resource Planing Systems using the organisational Learning Model. *International Journal of Management, 25*(2), 348-353.

Tucker, P. D., & Stronge, J. H. (2005). *Linking Teacher Evaluation and Student Learning.* Alexandria, USA: Association for Supervision and Curriculum Development.

Ulrich, D. (2008). HR Dreams: Where Human Resource is Headed to Deliver Value. In R. Galavan, J. Markides, & C. Murray, *Strategy, innovation and Change: Challenges in Managment* (pp. 97-109). Oxford: OUP.

Unaeza, A., & Gioko, M. A. (2007). Science subject leadership in the enhancement of information communication technology (ICT) integration in project based learning (PBL). In J. Khaki, & Q. Safdar, *Educational Leadership in Pakistan: Ideals and Realities.* (pp. 252-279). Pakistan: Oxford University Press.

Valsiner, J., & Van de Veer, R. (2000). *The social mind. Construction of the idea.* . Cambridge UK: Cambridge university Press.

Van Buren, H. J. (2003). Boundaryless Careers and Employability Obligations. *Business Ethics Quarterly, 13*(2), 131–150.

Van Buren, H. J., & Greenwood, M. (2008). Enhancing Employee Voice: Are Voluntary Employer–Employee Partnerships Enough? *Journal of Business Ethics, 81*, 209–221.

Van de Bossche, P., Segers, M., & Jansen, N. (2010). Transfer of training: the role of feedback in supportive social networks. *International Journal of Training and Development, 14*(2), 81-94.

Van Sell, M., Brief, A. P., & & Schuler, R. S. (1981). Role conflict and role ambiguity: Integration of the literature and directions for future research. *Human Relations, 34*(1), 43-71.

Velada, R., Caetano, A., Michel, J. W., & Kavanagh, M. J. (2007). The effects of training design, individual characteristics and work environment on transfer of training. *International Journal of Training and Development, 11*(4), 282-294.

Walker, R. (1983). Three good reasons for not doing a case study in curriculum research. *Journal of Curriculum Studies, 15*(2), 155-165.

Walsham, G. (2002). What can knowledge managment system deliver. *Management Communication Quarterly*, 267-273.

Wango, G. (2009). *School administration and management: Quality assurance and standards in schools.* Nairobi: Jomo Kenyatta Foundation.

Wellington, J. (2000). *Educational research: Contemporary issues and practical approaches.* London: Continuum.

White, C. (2004). *Strategic Management.* New York: Palgrave Macmillan.

Whittington, R. (2001). *What is Strategy and Does it Matter.*

Yamnill, S., & McLean, G. N. (2001). Theories supporting transfer of training. *Human Resource Development Quarterly, 12*(2), 195-208.

Yazici, H. J. (2009.). The Role of Project Management Maturity and Organisational Culture in Perceived Performance. *Project Management Journal, 40*(3), 14 – 33.

Yin, R. K. (2003). *Case study research.* . Thousand Oaks: CA Sage.

Yin, Y. K. (2009). *Case Study Research: Design and Methods.* Thousands Oaks, CA: Sage.

Zhu, Z., & Heady, R. B. (1994). A simplified method of evaluating PERT/CPM network parameters. *IEEE Transaction on Engineering Management., 41*, 426-430.

Printed in the United States
By Bookmasters